SENSE AND SPIRITUALITY

To dearest Gina,

With much love

from

Anita
xxx

Sense and Spirituality

THE ARTS AND SPIRITUAL FORMATION

James McCullough

CASCADE *Books* · Eugene, Oregon

SENSE AND SPIRITUALITY
The Arts and Spiritual Formation

Cascade Books
A Division of Wipf and Stock Publishers
199 W. 8th Ave., Suite 3
Eugene, OR 97401

www.wipfandstock.com

ISBN 13: 978-1-62564-921-8

Cataloging-in-Publication data:

McCullough, James, February 20, 1964–.

Sense and spirituality : the arts and spiritual formation / James McCullough, with a foreword by David Brown.

xxii + 124 p. ; 23 cm. Includes bibliographical references.

ISBN 13: 978-1-62564-921-8

1. Christianity and the arts. 2. Spiritual formation. 3. Spirituality. I. Brown, David, 1948 July 1–. II. Title.

BR115.A8 M119 2015

Manufactured in the U.S.A.

This book is for

Lydia Marie
Patrick James
Peter Joseph
and
Loryn Monica Meredith

Vi et Animo

Diligens et Fidus

Both of these mottoes are ascribed to what is claimed to be our family coat of arms. It may be true or a bit o' Hiberno-blarney, but in any case both mottoes are commendable, and I find all four qualities in all four of you.

Art is an antidote against any kind of superficiality, and perhaps against superficial spirituality most of all.

DAVID BAILY HARNED, *THEOLOGY AND THE ARTS*

Contents

Foreword

Unlike most researchers, the author came to work on a doctorate at St. Andrews with already considerable experience behind him in campus ministry and in university teaching and administration. So far from the resultant age difference being a disadvantage, it gave a depth to his reflections that they might not otherwise have had, not least because his chosen topic was spiritual formation and how the visual arts might contribute to such ongoing discipleship. It is no exaggeration to say that most viewers think art appreciation a relatively simple matter of like or dislike, with the meaning and significance of a particular painting easily deciphered in a relatively short space of time. Indeed, as one watches tourists race through major galleries snapping their cameras as they go, one wonders if the intention is simply to prove a particular viewing rather than to really engage with the painting in question. Jim McCullough rightly rejects such a shallow approach, insisting not only that there is much more involved for proper aesthetic appreciation but that sustained viewing can also reap profound spiritual rewards in increased religious self-understanding. As he puts it, ascesis (spiritual training) can work hand in hand with aesthesis (art perception). At St. Andrews he spent much of his time working through the practical implications of such a claim in respect of two major contemporary artists, the Scottish painter Peter Howson and the American artist Makoto Fujimura: wise choices, as their artwork could not be more different, the former being a representational artist and the latter working mainly with abstract forms. The result was that McCullough not only became an expert on the two artists but was also able to demonstrate how, irrespective of the form of the art, it could be used to develop Christian discipleship (both artists are themselves Christian). Meditations needed to be directed, but at the same time open, so that self-discovery could be an important element in the process. It was a technique that he employed with a number of student groups to remarkable effect.

In what follows, however, the main focus is on the theory behind such practice, and that too is important. While the twentieth century saw a marked growth of interest in the visual arts among more Protestant and Evangelical Christians, it would be true to say that an element of suspicion remained. Art could at most illustrate the truths of Scripture. Here Jim McCullough tries (successfully in my view) to take us well beyond such a position. Reflection on, and contemplation of, particular works of art has the power to deepen our understanding of the Christian faith. In this project he harnessed a number of scholars to his aid, most notably among them David Baily Harned. The result is that readers will learn as much about the views of other major writers in the field as they will be carried along (hopefully) by the skill of McCullough's own arguments and the obvious enthusiasm he demonstrates. Reading about theoretical foundations for particular practices can of course be at times difficult and even frustrating, but readers will soon be relieved by the clarity of McCullough's exposition, as by the admirable way in which he draws out the practical implications of what he proposes. Nor should the originality of what he writes be discounted. There are plenty of Christian books on moral formation, but here with aesthetic formation we are onto much rarer, and I believe highly fruitful, ground.

David Brown
Institute for Theology, Imagination and the Arts (ITIA)
St. Mary's College
University of St. Andrews

Preface

The writing of books is the cause of the accumulation of debts, debts of friendship, assistance, and support.

I want to start with those who kindly read portions or all of the manuscript of this book as I completed it. In this regard I want to begin with James Sire. I have known Jim for thirty years. His books, like *The Universe Next Door* (InterVarsity Press), were staples of my intellectual and theological development. Jim read through an early draft of this project. I continue to learn from him, and have appreciated his encouragement. Others who read and assisted me in the production of this book include Russ Wills, George Harne, Matthew Milliner.

David Brown, Professor of Theology, Aesthetics and Culture and Wardlaw Professor at the University of St. Andrews, was my doctoral supervisor and read draft after draft of my dissertation, which is the basis for this book. I could not have asked for a better guide in the completion of my degree or a more encouraging colleague. Both he and Ann Loades were wonderful friends to me and my family during our sojourn in Scotland.

My time in Scotland included meeting many people who were so kind to me and my family. I think of Trevor and Rachel Hart, Alice Tynte-Irvine, Gordon Methven, Mark Rust, Alice McLaughlin, and Elaine Miller.

Friends who have seen me through ups and downs since my return from Scotland include Ed Davis, Ralph Bingham, Barbara Charalambidis, Jennifer Lee, the aforementioned George Harne and Matthew Milliner, Rev. Hugh Brown, Rev. Marvin Foltz, Don

and Sherie Zimmer, Kathy Burge-Curtis, Jim Brix, and Garland
Pollard.

Much thanks to Robin Parry and Laura Poncy at Wipf &
Stock for all their editorial work.

As we all do, I began in a family and will conclude these ac-
knowledgements with my family. My mother, Joyce Funk, has sup-
ported me in so many ways and none so much as her unflagging
confidence in me. She has simply never doubted—as I certainly
did—that I would complete my degree or finish this book. My
father provides Irish humor and encouragement. My broth-
ers, Chad, George, Sonny, and Sean, are always affirming of me.
I conclude, of course, with appreciation for Gillian and our four
children. Lydia, Patrick, Peter, and Loryn are the center of my joy
in this world and continually let me know that they believe in me. I
believe in them even more. To them this book is dedicated.

Introduction

The text before you is an effort on my part to advance theological thinking about the arts in human life. In particular it is an effort to bring two different disciplines—theological aesthetics and practical theology—into dialogue around the theme of the relationship between the arts and spiritual formation. If this volume were to find a place on the shelves of practical theology its author would be very gratified, because it is directed toward *praxis* in the Christian life and with Christian laity primarily in mind.

Of the arts, music is the one with which I am most familiar and experienced. I studied music education as an undergraduate in college. At the same time that I was discovering music, which for me was primarily Western classical music, I was discovering life as a Christian. The two went very much hand in hand. A great enthusiasm for Shakespeare was also a part of my adolescent cosmos, as well as what would seem a natural enthusiasm for movies. Interwoven in my Christian experience were familiar features of church life that have aesthetic implications. I immediately think of rhetoric (public speaking, teaching, the liturgical reading of Scripture), church architecture, and hymnody. My primary youth experience being in the Methodist Church, hymns played a particularly strong role. It has become clearer to me over the years how deeply interwoven these dynamics of imaginative and expressive aspects religion and aesthetics were in my own development.

This pattern continued into my college years where I was a member of an evangelical parachurch fellowship. It was through this involvement that I was introduced to the concept of *worldview*, something that then became a central point around which so much of my developing mind and spirituality coalesced. It remains so for me today. The term is sometimes criticized for lacking philosophical rigor and definitional precision, but it is its very elasticity that makes it practically useful. Worldview as a category is large enough to encompass a collection of enthusiasms: God and theology, classical music and theater, literature and film, ethics and apologetics, politics and evangelism, racial reconciliation and resistance to the "culture of death." The concept of worldview, and the basically Reformed theology that sponsored much of the material that I was digesting during my undergraduate days, taught me that all these things and more found a center of gravity in the claim that God was sovereign over all things by virtue of creation and redemption. This provided me with theological permission to explore these things with a clear conscience, and the style of evangelism in which I was immersed gave permission, as it were, for a cautiously critical, risk-taking approach to the things of culture, art, and society.

Ten years of college campus ministry, followed by seminary training, further encouraged me in the integration of all things around the knowledge of God, and that knowledge of God issued in and called for a life of continuous transformation, and that this transformation again implicated all areas of life, the personal and public, the intellectual and affective, the propositional and the aesthetic. Another ten years of continued college ministry and teaching a variety of courses at the undergraduate level, followed by experience of pursuing a PhD in theology in a program of theological aesthetics has, I hope, prepared me to now give a more coherent and perhaps compelling account of what I believe to be the relationship between at least two aspects of this lifelong kaleidoscope of passions: the arts and spirituality.

It becomes difficult for me to know how, and what, the value of doing so would even be, of separating and labeling these different dynamics in some hermetically sealed manner. Thought and feeling, interior mulling and public expression, doctrine and decorum, poetry and prose, transparent proposition and allusive symbolism, signs and the signified, all converge in the formation of a spiritual existence, and I know that this is not my experience alone.

This project is an attempt, modest and incomplete as it is, to better understand the involution and mutual informing of these elements and dynamics of Christian spirituality, and perhaps in doing so find ways that might even better harness their potentials.

Professional Accountability

A blind reviewer of a version of this material questioned what academic field this project considers itself accountable to; that is, what area of expertise it reflects and which guild it submits itself to for approval or approbation. My response would be, first and foremost, to the growing body of scholars and practitioners in the field of theological aesthetics. A growing body of publications and academic programs has taken shape over the past twenty years that have advanced what Jeremy Begbie calls the "theology-arts conversation" to which he has contributed so much over this time period.[1] It is to my friends and colleagues who make up this field of study that I make myself primarily accountable. That the reviewer wondered where the project might academically situate itself may reflect the distance still to go in establishing theological aesthetics as a normal field of theological study.

Secondly, I welcome the critical consideration of those in practical theology. I think in particular of friends and colleagues such as Professor Lisa M. Hess at the United Theological Seminary. Two of Lisa's books, *Artisanal Theology* and *Learning in a Musical Key: Insight for Theology in Performative Mode* reflect the growing presence of the aesthetic within practical theology discourse.

---

1. Jeremy Begbie, "Jeremy Begbie on Beauty," www.transpositions. co.uk/2013/04/jeremy-begbie-on-beauty. The renaissance to which I refer, while not exclusively a Protestant phenomena, is what I am particularly thinking of when I write the above. Roman Catholicism and Eastern Orthodoxy have had a longer and less fraught relationship with the aesthetic in their respective traditions, while members of the Protestant communion, particularly within its Evangelical wing, have taken matters related to theology and the arts to a whole new level of discourse and consideration.

Thirdly, I welcome comments from my colleagues in the field of public theology. Like theological aesthetics, public theology has come into its professional own over the past thirty years. Represented now by a growing list of publications, an impressive international journal, and practitioners working at various institutions, public theology represents the task of exploring and guiding the mutual accountability of religion and civil society. Part of this mutual interface and influence lies in the area of the arts, and part of my wider arena of research involves the question of how the arts are forms of public theology. That emphasis is not the focus of attention in this project, but it does lie just beneath the surface of nearly all my reflections here.

But let me repeat that above all this is a project of theological aesthetics. Perhaps this appeal both calls for and would benefit from some definitional explication. Aidan Nichols, one of the key figures in the renaissance of aesthetics within Christian theology, succinctly defines theological aesthetics as that area of theological inquiry that "consider[s] the part played by the senses—with their associated powers of memory and imagination—in the awareness of God."[2] Much more can be said, obviously, but Nichols captures what I take to be of the essence of theological aesthetics, namely inquiry into the relationship between the sensory and the spiritual. The issue of beauty has a role to play in this inquiry, and has occupied a central place in both theological and philosophical aesthetics, as well as the practice of aesthetics, for a long time. This project does not contribute anything substantial to questions of beauty, that is, to questions of canon, criteria, presence or absence, etc. The emphasis here is on what might be called the *rhetoric* of the arts; that is, what art is, how it carries meaning, and what all this might have to do with the phenomenon of spiritual formation. Persuasion, analyzed in a particularly narrative mode, is what occupies center stage in this project. The arts are analyzed as modes of communication, and questions of beauty are regulated to a secondary level of consideration.[3]

2. Nichols, *A Key to Balthasar*, 14.

3. There are many valuable texts which address the matter of beauty in art

My account of the persuasiveness of the arts, the rhetorical dynamic on which this project dwells, involves an analysis rendered in a Venn diagram of overlapping circles. As will be explained, this is done for heuristic purposes and inevitably involves the kind of artificial distinctions required for analysis, but hidden in actual practice. The reviewer to whom I referred above wondered if I wasn't engaged in unnecessary generalities and guilty of a kind of confusion of categories in the construction of my theory. I leave it to the reader to be the final judge of these concerns. My theory of what art is, its ontological status if you will, rests on what I identify as its three irreducible elements, or dimensions, without which there is no "art" and the awareness of which assists one in hearing what art is "saying."

I do make a claim in these pages that perhaps should be stated as clearly as possible, to be given elaboration in what follows. I maintain that *the arts are modes of communication, rendered or expressed in distinct types of "languages" which are embedded in time, culture, worldview, and traditions of development*. As I will state in what follows, while works of art cannot and should not be reduced to singular, detachable "messages," artworks always communicate some sense of life, a perspective on things. It is in attending with ever-greater sensitivity and openness to this communicative dynamic at the heart of art that I maintain spiritual formation can really takes place. For that reason, I engage in a heuristic project that includes graphs and diagrams in order to help the inquisitive and intelligent lay reader of these pages, to whom it is primarily addressed, better encounter the world of the arts in all its forms and functions.

and theology; see Richard Harries, *Art and the Beauty of God*; Edward Farley, *Faith and Beauty: A Theological Aesthetic*; Patrick Sherry, *Spirit and Beauty*, 2nd ed. The work of Frank Burch Brown deserves particular mention in regards to recent work within Protestant theology on the relationship of beauty, the arts and religion; see *Religious Aesthetics* and *Good Taste, Bad Taste, and Christian Taste: Aesthetics in Religious Life*. A kind of magnum opus in this area of research would be David Bentley Hart's *The Beauty of the Infinite: The Aesthetics of Christian Truth*. My regard for this formidable exploration of the question of beauty as a necessary category in theology and Christian life is tempered only by its obscurity of expression.

Theology is an inherently interdisciplinary undertaking. This project reflects that interdisciplinary dynamic. The disciplines that this project makes contact with include aesthetics, in both philosophical and theological forms of inquiry, epistemology, rhetoric, hermeneutics, ethics, practical theology, and spiritual theology. The footnotes accompanying the text and the bibliography will reflect the range of sources used in the writing of this book. In almost every case I reflect these readings in order to provide further sources for the reader and as a commendation of those sources. Moreover the text includes the occasional "excursus" where I highlight some aspect of the argument or concept or personality involved in the argument. These also serve to put things on the reader's "radar" that might lead toward further fruitful reading or research.

This book began its life as a doctoral dissertation, and as happens with most dissertations that are published, this one has undergone extensive editing and rewriting in order to make it readable and indeed palatable for a general audience. One of the happier aspects of that original research for me was the discovery of the work of David Baily Harned. Harned's own career began with his dissertation, entitled *Theology and the Arts*, published in 1966.[4] He went on to make a modest but significant contribution to Christian ethics between the late 1960s into the 1990s, advancing a basically Barthian theology, but inflected with a sensitive awareness of the aesthetic dimensions of ethics and religion and a moral realist concern to interpret the present in light of theological conviction and ethical responsibility. With the recent reissue of his first book that contribution stands to continue.

I was introduced to the name of David Baily Harned with a citation from his book *Faith and Virtue*. Here Harned advanced his conviction that all moral and religious activity revolves around one's capacity to "see." Obviously this is meant in a wholistic, metaphorical sense, as the visually impaired are clearly capable of such moral sight. But the conviction remains and has inherently aesthetic implications, as Harned writes about in nearly all

---

4. Harned, *Theology and the Arts* (1966, reissued 2014).

his publications. The quotation with which I was first introduced to Harned's work remains central to the development of my own work and the argument of this project:

> Our worldly ways reflect the world as we see it; we are free to act in some purposive fashion only within the world that we can see. Before our decisions, supporting our approach to moral life, distinguishing us from our neighbors, there is our way of seeing. But it is not easy to see, no easier than it is to listen, to hear not what we would like, not what we would expect, not only what the language means, but what intention and anguish and hope are veiled as well as disclosed by the recalcitrance of words. Seeing is never simply a reaction to what passes before our eyes; it is a matter of how well the eye is trained and provisioned to discern the richness and the terror, beauty and banality, of the worlds outside and within the self.[5]

5. Harned, *Faith and Virtue*, 29.

Part I

Theoretical Framework

1

The Arts and Spirituality

What is the place of art in the Christian life? Is art—
especially the fine arts of painting and music—simply a
way to bring in worldliness through the back door? We
know that poetry may be used to praise God in, say, the
psalms and maybe even in modern hymns. But what
about sculpture or drama? Do these have any place in
the Christian life? Shouldn't a Christian focus his gaze
steadily on "religious things" alone and forget about art
and culture?[1]

Recent Reflections on the Arts and Christianity

The anxieties given expression in the passage above seem one-
sided now, even among those who identify with conservative
forms of Christian faith. While concerns about worldliness
remain, a more confident posture toward matters of art and culture have largely, although not entirely, replaced former feelings
of insecurity and alienation. Among Evangelicals in the English-
speaking world, the arguments and anxieties have turned toward
questions related to what kind of art is beneficial, how art might
be effectively deployed for religious purposes, and how the arts
might be more meaningfully engaged. But when the influential

1. Schaeffer, *Art and the Bible*, 7.

American Evangelical Francis Schaeffer wrote his tract *Art and the Bible* in 1973, such anxieties and misgivings were very much at the forefront.

Much has happened since Schaeffer in effect gave Evangelicals permission to engage with matters of art and culture. Evangelicals and Christians of all communions have in the ensuing years produced a wealth of studies addressing the relationship between the arts and Christian faith, theology, mission, and imagination. There seems to be no abatement of this trend. Just a few very recent examples might suffice to substantiate this claim.

Nancy Pearcey is a direct intellectual and theological descendent of Francis Schaeffer. In her 2010 book *Saving Leonardo: A Call to Resist the Secular Assault on Mind, Morals, and Meaning*, she extends Schaeffer's cautiously positive regard for the arts, particularly as they serve as both signs and symptoms of trends within Western society. The book is a welcome contribution to otherwise familiar "worldview" analyses of culture that tend to focus almost exclusively on human thinking as opposed to human doing, making, or feeling. Her reflections on the arts as forms of "language" that project ideational content is a perspective shared in this project. But there are disappointing limitations to the scope of her analysis. Her approach to the arts is largely predetermined along a narrow set of criteria, and the manner in which artworks are portrayed as one-dimensionally "true" or "false" tends towards the sense of a lack of depth. A similar narrowness of theological and doctrinal orientation, where a basically neo-Reformed Evangelicalism passes muster as the "Christianity" against which all other forms or faiths are measured, adds to the narrowness of cultural engagement.[2]

By contrast Timothy J. Gorringe offers a quite different perspective. In *Earthly Visions: Theology and the Challenges of Art*,

2. Daniel Siedell offers an excellent critique from an Evangelical perspective of such facile analyses of art in *God in the Gallery: A Christian Embrace of Modern Art*. Another appreciative but insightfully critical review of recent Evangelical analysis of the arts is found in James Watkin's review of Jerram Barrs' *Echoes of Eden: Reflections on Christianity, Literature, and the Arts*, http://www.transpositions.co.uk/2014/05/review-echoes-of-eden/.

Gorringe, like Pearcey, seeks to address the presence and meaning of the "secular" in Western society. Unlike Pearcey, however,
Gorringe does not locate changes in perception and orientation
in a one-dimensional story of decline. Gorringe sees Western
secularism—that is, the affirmation of the value and validity of the
temporal world—as a logical outcome of Western Christianity,
especially its Protestant variety. In support of this thesis, Gorringe
refreshingly explores some of the less familiar works of the Dutch
School, still life, portraiture, and abstraction, paintings where the
things of this world assume center stage. Employing an undevel-
oped metaphor from Karl Barth, Gorringe suggests that works
such as these can be interpreted theologically as "secular parables."
It is a compelling thesis argued in a persuasive manner, with the
added virtue of introducing readers to aspects of Western art too
often overlooked in such analyses.

The most impressive recent project of theology and the arts,
in terms of sheer size and extent of engagement, is David Brown's
three-volume series published by Oxford University Press.[3]
Brown's agenda for the entire series is to "widen the range of material thought relevant to constructive theology," particularly in the
realms of cultivated nature, the arts, and human activity.[4] Brown's
repeated admonition that Christians should first engage in careful
"listening," rather than anxiously predetermining potential meanings in art and culture, is a helpful balance to what too often takes
place.

My project responds to and seeks to expand on two of Brown's
contributions. One is his thesis on the sacramental potentials of
art. Brown bases this thesis on the theological presupposition
that God is "generous" and desires to make himself accessible and
available for human finding, and that God does so both within and
from without the specifically Christian circle of influence. Brown's

---

3. The three volumes are *God and Enchantment of Place*, *God and Grace
of Body*, and *God and Mystery in Words*. If linked with two previous volumes,
Tradition and Imagination and *Discipleship and Imagination*, then a project of
five volumes in length can be considered.

4. Brown, *God and Enchantment of Place*, 1.

recourse to the sacramental is grounded on the analogy of what God accomplishes in the life, death, and resurrection of Jesus, which is extended to being perceived as "a major, and perhaps even the primary, way of exploring God's relationship to our world."[5] A sacrament for Brown is both a sign and a real extension of God's presence in the world made available to human understanding and experience. Like Gorringe's use of the parabolic, Brown's analysis of the arts and human culture within a sacramental paradigm has the virtue of placing the "secular" aspects of life within a "sacred" scope of perception. They highlight the efforts of rendering genuinely theological analyses of these natural and human phenomena. My concern with the invocation of the sacramental in an analysis of art, however, is the degree that it implicates God in products of human endeavor, at least when the object under consideration is a work of art. Again, part of the effort of this essay is to allow works of art to have their own integrity as human artifacts. Humans are traditionally understood to be made in God's image, and operate within a context of God's creating and redeeming purposes, and even their best and most original works are but derivative of God's creative properties. But I wish to move slowly on the attribution of these works to God's intentions.

Drawing on a variety of resources my project advances the paradigm of the *catalyst* as a way to understand the relationship between the arts and spirituality. The paradigm of the catalyst is less metaphysically fraught, less theologically loaded, and yet can address itself to the positive ways the arts might contribute to Christian spirituality. Indeed, even the most "secular" works, which on every other criteria of assessment might be deplorable in intention and disturbing in content, might serve to catalyze meaningful reflections on life with or apart from God, while making no particular claims on divine implication in the work.

Secondly, David Brown's project focuses on the *experiential*. His whole project centers on "reclaiming human experience" for its theological significance. The thrust of my project seeks to explore the *cumulative* effects of religiously significant experiences,

5. Ibid., 6.

namely those in relation to the aesthetic. Such experiences should result in something yielding lasting effects. I seek to understand those effects in terms of *spiritual formation*.

EXCURSUS

Francis A. Schaeffer (1912–84)

Francis Schaeffer was what might be called a cultural evangelist and apologist, who maintained a high-profile ministry from the late 1960s till his death in 1984. Among his achievements was a series of lectures that were turned into books that highlighted the intersections of cultural and theological matters. Schaeffer identified religious and philosophical implications of art. He received tutorial help in this endeavor from the Dutch art critic and historian Hans Rookmaaker (1922–77), and so advanced among Anglo-American Evangelicals a Reformed "worldview" analysis of art. He is credited with inspiring a greater sense of cultural confidence among conservative Evangelicals.

Art as Communication

Like the projects reviewed above, this one also rests on certain theological convictions. It is assumed, on the basis of a certain reading of Scripture and the Christian tradition, that God's intentions in relation to humans is for communion: a relationship analogous to friendship, but closer to marriage, mystical in character, practical in output, and which, in the words of one theologian, "requires and releases" capacities commensurate for such a relationship and shared mission in the world. A theology so centered on communion might be expected to raise the category of *communication* to a rather high level, and indeed this project does so. If "In the beginning was the *Logos*," it can be argued that this issues not only in words, but in intentions of communication ordered to *communio*: a communion that Christian theology sees existing in the life of the Trinity and that extends from the Trinity to humanity. In this reading, humanity in God's image is *homo communicator*, humanity the communicator, and in this light "true art" is that which "*speaks* and receives the world in one integral movement of generosity and gratitude."[6]

Art as *poesis* is, of course, human making. But there are some forms of human making that transcend immediate and practical usage and become, and were intended to be, acts of communication; human doing becomes human saying. The exact liminal point wherein such making becomes saying cannot always be ascertained, but this project advances the thesis that art is best understood as a dynamic of *how* something is done (craft), *what* it renders (content), and *why* it was so conceived and executed (context).

Communication, then, lies at the heart of this project. The arts are, in this report, communicative acts of making and performing with the immediate or cumulative effect of story, *mythos*, "world-projection," "worldmaking," worldview. To learn the "language" of a given work and break through to a meaningful connection with the artwork, the artist or tradition from which the artwork emerges is to encounter the story being projected in it, and it is the dynamic of story that insinuates a truth-claim upon the receiver, a truth-claim that can be accepted, rejected, considered, or "indwelt" by the receiver which alters not only one's moral vision of things, but one's very capacity to alter such vision. *Eyesight* (standing here for any form of aesthetic encounter) becomes *insight*, and the arts, as argued in the following pages, are an effective catalyst for this dynamic process.[7]

6. Gorringe, *Earthly Vision: Theology and the Challenges of Art*, 2, quoting Hart, *The Beauty of the Infinite*.

7. Miles, *Image as Insight*, 2, citing Rudolf Arnheim, *Art and Visual Perception*, 31. For the purposes of this study I am content with an understanding of beauty as a "compelling presence," a "persuasive attraction" that invites attention without coercing it. I am perfectly content with Arnheim's terse definition: "Aesthetic beauty is the isomorphic correspondence between what is said and how it is said." (Arnheim, *Visual Thinking*, 255.)

The reader will note an emphasis on the ideational dimension of the arts in this project. The cognitive aspect of aesthetic experience is emphasized in part because of the way the arts are too often reduced to the emotional or sensual values attached to them. This project contributes to the claim that the arts represent alternate ways of *knowing*, and thereby afford opportunities to grow in *understanding*. The arts also provide opportunities to develop and hone skills analogous to *contemplation*. This project is replete with references to attentiveness, careful observation, open-mindedness, deferral of judgment, and the like, capacities required to engage in and maintain a relationship with a work of art are analogous to and exist, as argued here, in dialectical relationship with those capacities required for progressive development in spirituality. Taking advantage of the alliterative opportunity afforded by two Greek words, an earlier form of this project expressed its reflections on the relationship between the arts and spiritual formation in terms of *aesthesis* and *ascesis*.[8] *Aesthesis* refers to sensory perception and, by extension, its contribution to the development of the *imagination*. *Ascesis* originated as an athletic term, but was adopted for the disciplines associated with progressive growth in spirituality.[9] Similarly alliterative but perhaps less obscure, I now employ the terms *sense* and *spirituality*.[10] My agenda remains the same, however; that is, to explore how skills in sensory perception and imaginative engagement exist in a dialectical relationship with those related to ascetical development or spiritual formation, and how this dialectical relationship can be mediated, enhanced, or *catalyzed* through encounters with the arts.

---

8. McCullough, "*Aesthesis* and *Ascesis*: The Relationship between the Arts and Spiritual Formation," PhD dissertation, 2013.

9. 1 Cor 9:24–27. See Allen, *Spiritual Theology*, 67; Sheldrake, *Spirituality and History*, 52–56; see also Thornton, *English Spirituality*, 35.

10. For the aesthetic meaning of "sense," see Lewis, *Studies in Words*, 133f.

Defining Spirituality and Spiritual Formation

Spirituality is a central concept in this project and deserves to be defined before we proceed further. Scholars seeking to define Christian spirituality typically make recourse to biblical, doctrinal, theological, and more recently, psychological, philosophical, phenomenological, anthropological, and sociological resources.[11] Nelson Thayer, for example, writes that "'spirituality' is a term whose meaning is at once evident and elusive."[12] His study focuses on the development of a pastoral theology of spirituality, and in his review relies strongly on the contributions of the psychoanalytic tradition, exegetical studies of relevant biblical terminology, and the phenomenology of religion as experienced by the subject. Drawing from definitions of spirituality in works of pastoral theology, Thayer notes the occurrence of words and phrases such as "transcendent," "relationship towards," "integration," "context." In an attempt at a synthesis, Thayer issues his own working definition:

> Spirituality is the specifically human capacity to experience, be conscious of, and relate to a dimension of power and meaning transcendent to the world of sensory reality expressed in the particularities of a given historical and social context, and leads towards action congruent with its meaning.[13]

In an article exploring recent studies on the relationship between spirituality and healthcare, Philip Sheldrake notes the "deconstruction" of traditional connections between institutional religion and personal development. Spirituality in this context

11. Among the most widely cited in nearly all the subsequent scholarly literature on the concept of "spirituality" and its subsequent reemergence in Western theology in the mid-twentieth century is Walter Principe, "Toward Defining Spirituality"; see also Principe, "Theological Trends: Pluralism in Christian Spirituality." See also Wiseman, *Spirituality and Mysticism: A Global View*, 1–20, which helpfully incorporates Principe's scholarship within a framework of more recent research, and also Cunningham and Egan, *Christian Spirituality: Themes from the Tradition*, 9–28.

12. Thayer, *Spirituality and Pastoral Care*, 31.

13. Ibid., 55.

comes to mean anything to anybody.[14] In response to these ten-
dencies Sheldrake writes that while he would not want to reduce
spirituality strictly to the content of belief, nonetheless:

> "spirituality" does imply a world-view, that is, a vision
> of the human spirit and what will assist it to achieve
> its full potential. So, in that sense, some kind of belief
> is implicit in all forms of spirituality even if it is largely
> unexamined.[15]

The word "spirituality" remains useful for speaking generally
about the intersecting dynamics of the cognitive, affective, and even
psychomotor dimensions of religious life. "Spiritual formation," on
the other hand, invokes a concept with greater specification and
meaning. The phrase is itself a metaphor for the assimilation of
qualities and capacities necessary for participation in a life with
God.[16] The phrase is useful for its familiarity within the Christian
community for communicating a sense of goal-orientation in
spirituality. Such language of formation in relation to Christianity
finds validation in the text of the New Testament, particularly in
Paul's letters:

---

14. Sheldrake, "Spirituality and Healthcare," 368.

15. Ibid., 377. Examples of definitions could be continued at great length.

16. The language employed here is fairly standard. In regards to my usage
of "capacity" in relation to spirituality, I see it as related to matters of both
cognition and ability, as articulated in the following:

> Intelligence is defined as a group of mental abilities. An ability (of any
> sort), in turn, is a characteristic of an individual when that individual can
> "successfully complete (i.e. obtain a specific, desired, outcome on) a task
> of defined difficulty, when testing conditions are favorable." . . . From this
> perspective, mental ability is synonymous with mental *capacity*, similar to
> mental skill (which specifically connotes something learned), and similar
> to mental competence, which emphasizes the ability to meet a specific
> standard.

Mayer, Salovey, and Caruso, "Emotional Intelligence as Zeitgeist, as Personality,
and as Mental Ability" in Bar-On and Parker, eds., *The Handbook of Emotional
Intelligence*, 105. Emphasis added.

GALATIANS 4:19

My little children, for whom I am again in the pain of
childbirth until Christ is formed (*morphothé*) in you . . .

ROMANS 8:29

For those whom he foreknew he also predestined to be
conformed (*summórphous*) to the image of his Son . . .

ROMANS 12:2

Do not be conformed to this world, but be transformed
(*metamorphoústhe*) by the renewing of your minds, so
that you may discern what is the will of God . . .

2 CORINTHIANS 3:18

And all of us . . . are being transformed (*metamorphoú-
metha*) into the same image from one degree of glory to
another . . .

All of these passages employ words based on the root *morphé* or
"form," a term used principally in relation to a physical characteristic, but which is here applied to progressive change in character
and moral existence.

In the entry for "Spiritual Formation" in a recently published dictionary of Christian spirituality, the article begins by
recognizing that the phrase historically has been associated with
the preparation of clergy. Spiritual or priestly formation refers to
what developed as the period of training that involved religious
disciplines and education in biblical studies, preaching, and
liturgical leadership. The tradition also developed distinctions between ascetical and mystical theologies, now generally subsumed
together under the heading of spiritual theology. The article notes
the increasing professionalization and psychologization of these
processes over the past hundred years. Towards the conclusion
the article addresses the subject matter in its more contemporary
context in reference to practices such as retreats, sabbaticals, and
catechesis, and provides material for a working definition:

But religious belief cannot be divorced from the context of life experience. Through the power of desire and symbolic imagination, the thoughtful human being is always exercised by the gap between ordinary human capacity and what she or he may feel drawn to achieve. Spiritual formation becomes a strategy, within the religious impulse, for addressing this moral gap and achieving the radical transformation of the self. While the interior journey, in a secular sense, has self-awareness as its goal, the spiritual journey leads to self-awareness in relationship to God, and under the transformative power of grace. It is the regular practice of the spiritual life in prayer and the virtues, as well as education in the insights of the human sciences, that constitute spiritual formation as the solid grounding for the following of Christ.[17]

In a similar vein, George Lindbeck offered the following description of spiritual formation:

> Looked at non-theologically, spiritual formation may be described as the deep and personally committed appropriation of a comprehensive and coherent outlook on life and the world. From this perspective, those who are maturely humanistic or maturely Marxist, for example, are in their own way spiritually well-formed. The spiritually mature are not simply socialized into behaving under standard conditions as is expected of members of their group, but they have to a significant degree *developed the capacities and dispositions to think, feel, and act in accordance with their world view* no matter what the circumstances. They have, in Aristotelian language, the habits or virtues distinctively emphasised by the encompassing vision which is theirs. In the Christian case, these are traditionally named faith, hope and love, but

---

17. Simmonds, "Spiritual Formation," in Philip Sheldrake, ed., *The New SCM Dictionary of Christian Spirituality*, 330. Diogenes Allen provides an account of how classical ascetical theology, such as found in Evagrius and John Cassian, provide guidelines for the assessment of spiritual progression and "strategies" for formation; *Spiritual Theology*, 64–67. See also Louth, *The Origins of the Christian Mystical Tradition*, 98–131.

other religions when internalized may involve quite a
different set of virtues.[18]

Practically speaking then, the question becomes how the arts
might play a role in the cultivation of "the power of desire," growth
in "symbolic imagination," and the development of "capacities and
dispositions to think, feel and act" in ways congruent with spiritual formation. My own work on the relationship between the arts
and spiritual formation places an emphasis on sense perception
and aesthetic sensitivity. Crucial in this working understanding
of formation is the scriptural injunction, occurring several times
throughout the Bible, of having *eyes that see and ears that hear.*[19]

Building a Theoretical Framework

Much has been written on the theological implications of art,
the aesthetic implications of theology, how the arts contribute to
religious tradition, and how the arts mediate encounter with the
divine. Not enough, perhaps, has directly addressed the relationship between the arts and what this project refers to as spiritual
formation.[20] Appreciative of the work of scholars in the field of
theological aesthetics, such as Gordon Graham, Frank Brown,
Jeremy Begbie, and Aidan Nichols, the theological ethics of David
Baily Harned, and insights from the practical theology of human
development as explored by the late James Loder, this project seeks
to advance what it considers a *critically realist* philosophy of art;
that is, critically realist *ontologically* in maintaining that things
have an objective existence and are related to one another by virtue of the doctrines of creation and redemption; critically realist
epistemologically in maintaining that we truly encounter a world

18. Lindbeck, "Spiritual Formation and Theological Education," 287.

19. See Mark 8:17–18, Isa 6:9, Rev 2:7f. For an excellent discussion of
spiritual formation and traditional Protestant concerns about the concept,
see Porter, "Sanctification in a New Key: Relieving Evangelical Anxieties over
Spiritual Formation," 129–48.

20. A recent exception would be Benner, *Contemplative Vision: A Guide to
Christian Art and Prayer.*

of reality outside of ourselves and can gain knowledge of these realities, but that this knowledge is nonetheless culturally and historically conditioned; and a critically realist *hermeneutically* in its approach to art, explored further in the next section.[21]

The argument of this book can be summarized along the following points:

1. Spiritual formation is the result of cumulative religious experiences, including experiences mediated by or in encounter with the arts.

2. The metaphor of the catalyst is adopted as one way of identifying how the arts facilitate spiritual formation. The arts catalyze spiritual formation by mediating the dynamics associated with aesthetical and ascetical practices. Dispositions conducive to meaningful encounters with art are analogous to those associated with religious dispositions associated with progress in spirituality, and vice 4versa.

3. An effective or meaningful encounter with art involves and perhaps requires an experience with art frequently characterized as "reading"; that is, gaining a sense of what an artwork is communicating.[22] This characterization further underlines the claim that the arts are conveyers of cognitively valuable content.

---

21. I am particularly indebted to N. T. Wright's explication of critical realism in his work in biblical hermeneutics and its applicability to other areas of knowledge. See *The New Testament and the People of God*, 35 ff.

22. Graham Howes articulates this characterization when he writes:

While many can, at least in theory, read scripture, relatively few can "read" paintings or stained-glass windows, and most recent revivals of faith and devotion—for example, Liberation Theology or Charismatic Renewal movements—have tended to be grounded in words rather than pictures. Indeed among many cultural and ecclesiastical elites the presumption is usually that while religious art may have some didactic, even aesthetic, value, it has no cognitive function. . . . Yet the central question remains. It is whether art is a way of seeing and knowing which is as truth-bearing in its way as philosophical and scientific method.

Howes answers his rhetorical question in the affirmative; *The Art of the Sacred*, 19.

4. Associated with the metaphor of "reading" is that of the "languages" of the arts. This project advances the metaphor of language to that of an analogy, and argues that the basic content of art is what this essay calls its *story*, not in the sense of a plotline, but in the sense of a mythic import or a worldview.

The relationship between sense and spirituality is the focus of this book. Exploring *how* these faculties, existing in dialectical relationship, issue in spiritual formation is the task of what follows, and here Francis Schaeffer is again of continuing influence for me. In the same tract cited at the beginning of this chapter, Schaeffer writes:

> Art forms add strength to the world view which shows through, no matter what the world view is or whether the world view is true or false. Think, for example, of a side of beef hanging in a butcher shop. It just hangs there. But if you go to the Louvre and look at Rembrandt's painting, "Side of Beef Hanging in a Butcher Shop," it's very different. It's startling to come upon this particular work because it says a lot more than its title. Rembrandt's art causes us to see the side of beef in a concentrated way, and, speaking for myself, after looking and looking at his picture, I have never been able to look a side of beef in a butcher shop with the superficiality I did before.[23]

Exploring how the arts cause one to see in a "concentrated way" and how by "looking and looking" one can break through "superficiality" towards meaning and change of perspective (and perhaps of life) is the theme we now set out to consider.

23. Schaeffer, *Art and the Bible*, 38. The painting is variously titled "The Slaughtered Ox," "The Flayed Ox," or "Carcass of Beef" and dated between 1655 and 1657. It is now in the Louvre collection.

FIGURE 1

Rembrandt van Rijn, *The Slaughtered Ox*, c. 1655, oil on canvas, 94 x 67 cm

EXCURSUS

Rembrandt van Rijn (1606–69)

Dutch artist of the Baroque period, he belonged to the prosperous Protestant society and many of his early and middle works are dedicated to subject matters which they would have found appealing and theologically acceptable. Many art critics note a more somber, introspective turn in Rembrandt's work following the death of his wife Saskia.

2

A Communicative Theory of the Arts

> What we encounter in all works of art are meaningful forms—visual, verbal, or audible—that communicate some kind of promise, project, or proposition that calls for our response and has the potential to affect us.[1]

In his book, *What Good Are the Arts?*, British literary scholar John Carey breaks down the title question into four separate points of inquiry: what a work of art is, whether "high art" is superior to "low art," whether art can make people morally better, and whether it can be a substitute for religion. While all four inquiries are relevant to this project, the first and third are central to it, and the differences between Carey's and my own conclusions are illuminating.

Carey approaches these questions in favor of a nonelitist and nonreligious point of view. Given this, it perhaps is not surprising that, after a review of the history and relevant literature of the history of aesthetics, Carey would conclude regarding the question of what art is:

> My answer to the question "What is a work of art?" is "A work of art is anything that anyone has ever considered a work of art, though it may be a work of art only for that one person."[2]

---

1. Vanhoozer, "Praising in Song: Beauty and the Arts," 114.
2. Carey, *What Good Are the Arts?* 29.

The merit of such an answer is its indeterminacy and democratic affinity. The problem is that it is really an expression of despair, a resignation of ever finding a categorical understanding of a significant human enterprise. And with regards to the matter of whether art can ever improve the human condition (and again, he thinks primarily in terms of the visual arts throughout), he is equally skeptical. Relying on examples drawn almost exclusively from contemporary art, particularly from the easily caricatured realm of conceptual art, Carey is by turns cynical and sarcastic in his dismissal of any claims of the "spirituality," "elevating," or idea-laden potentialities of the arts, with the exception of creative literature. His critique of the differences between high and low art focuses exclusively on the experiential differences noted by enthusiasts of either category. There is no consideration that the distinction might be based on relative differences of skill involved in different styles of art and that there might exist a basis to speak of "high" and "low" examples in all genre of art, including those identified as "popular." As to the question of the value or "spirituality" of a given work of art, this question is dismissed as uselessly arcane.

Carey finds no evidence, scientific or otherwise, that the arts improve human morality and concludes with what appears to have been his premise, that the arts, especially the bogeyman of the "high arts," are mere apertures of social class distinction. In contrast, however, Carey maintains that literature "develops and enlarges the mind" by virtue of what he finds to be its essential "indistinctness," that is, its open-endedness, which allows the reader to exercise greater imaginative faculties, while at the same time literature, unlike other arts, is, according to Carey, capable of self-critique, and therefore is neither indoctrinating nor contentless. Literature for Carey supplies the reader with something to think about as well as something to feel and engage with:

> It is that literature gives you ideas to think with. It stocks your mind. It does not indoctrinate, because diversity, counter-argument, reappraisal and qualification are its essence. But it supplies material for thought. Also,

because it is the only art capable of criticism, it encourages questioning, and self-questioning.[3]

Carey draws near to conclusion when he writes:

Poetic ideas do not tell you what the truth is, they make you feel what it would be like to know it. Because they make you feel as well as think, you can appropriate them, grow into them, adopt them as your own.[4]

Because for Carey other forms of art suffer from "indistinctness," they cannot achieve this level of cognitive and ethical efficacy for the receiver. That Carey fails to recognize that his positive assessment of literature might also apply to other forms of art as well is regrettable and can only be attributed either to ignorance or the influence of prejudice. Carey's book does, however, throw down a gauntlet to anyone setting out to provide an account for how art might somehow contribute to or facilitate religious formation. As to the question of what constitutes art, the inadequacy of Carey's answer is captured in Philip Sheldrake's study of what in the contemporary world is perhaps the equal in elusiveness, the matter of spirituality. For Sheldrake, spirituality, even given a multivalence of perspectives, must be subject to definition because, as he writes, if a given subject matter has "no conceptual limits, effectively it means nothing."[5]

In this chapter, I want to counter definitions of art such as Carey's with an account that explains what I believe to be the phenomenon of art. *Art is an act of human communication through practiced or embodied actions.* Connecting with a work of art or a performance, and perhaps by extension with the artist requires an understanding of what the art or artist is "doing," and that such an understanding constitutes an achievement in communication. It is not to suggest that works of art can, or even worse, should be reduced to singular, detachable "messages," but that the arts do in fact convey meaningful content, content that issues from and

3. Ibid., 208.

4. Ibid., 246.

5. Sheldrake, *Spirituality and History*, 40.

results in meaningful communication. It is a commonplace that the arts express emotions. The arts, it is argued here, also express *ideas*, ideas, as it has been said, that have consequences. That the arts have cognitive import, that they are means of understanding as well as of sensual delight, strengthens the claim that the arts can catalyze spiritual formation.

Philosophical Aesthetics

A good working understanding of art that both does justice to its complexity and can be articulated with simplicity would advance the cause of integrating art and theology. To this end the resources of philosophical aesthetics can be of great assistance. The history of philosophical aesthetics is made up of several major lines of thought regarding the understanding of artistic phenomena.[6] Under the influence of Romantic thought, the nineteenth and early twentieth centuries were dominated by what is usually referred to as expressivist theories of art, which held that art is primarily the expression of emotion and addresses itself the feelings of the receiver. Since the mid-twentieth century, aesthetic theories have digressed into various schools and have fell into exhaustion in the late sixties and seventies. Since then, however, fuelled in part by a revival of interest in aspects of traditional philosophy, philosophical aesthetics has witnessed a return to normative and definitional approaches to understanding art.

One of the challenges facing the contemporary theorist of art is the vast multiplicity of what passes for or is claimed to be art. Faced with so many examples of such wildly varying styles accompanied with an assortment of theoretical justifications, the theorist feels intimidated from offering any account of art that would be all-inclusive. Dennis Dutton's concern, for example, is that contemporary theorizing about art (he highlights such figures as George Dickie and the late Arthur Danto as representative

---

6. For a brief review of this history, see Dickie, *Art and Value*, 3–11.

cases) has become so overly anxious about "hard cases" that a kind of intellectual paralysis has set in:

> The obsession with accounting for art's most problematic outliers, while both intellectually challenging and a good way for teachers of aesthetics to generate discussion, has left aesthetics ignoring the center of art and its values. What philosophy of art needs is an approach that begins by treating art as a field of activities, objects, and experience given naturally in human life. We must first try to demarcate an uncontroversial center that gives outliers whatever interest they have.[7]

While not defining art per se, Dutton proceeds to advance a case for what he terms a "naturalistic" approach to art theory, based on the large, cross-culturally observable features of artistic phenomenon. To this end, Dutton presents what he terms "recognition criteria," based on what he perceives as "cross-culturally identified patterns of behaviour and discourse: the making, experiencing, and assessing of works of art."[8] Dutton's twelve criteria for identifying art are (1) direct pleasure, (2) skill or virtuosity, (3) style, (4) novelty or creativity, (5) criticism, (6) representation, (7) "special" focus, (8) expressive individuality, (9) emotional saturation, (10) intellectual challenge, (11) art traditions and institutions, (12) imaginative experience. Dutton does not claim that all art manifests these criteria, or that the list is exhaustive or not subject to alteration. It does, he proposes, establish a commonsense (my term) approach to art theory that might assist lay persons to attain better access and appreciation of the arts.[9] Work such as Dutton's helps establish a basis that the arts are *something* rather than *anything*.

While work such as Dutton's helps clear space for understanding in practical ways the phenomenon of art, what remains to

7. Dennis Dutton, quoted in Meskin, "From Defining Art to Defining the Individual Arts: The Role of Theory in the Philosophies of Arts," 137. See also Dutton, "A Naturalist Definition of Art," 367–77.

8. Ibid., 368.

9. Ibid., 369–73.

be addressed is how the arts might advance influence on its receivers. Answering this would also advance a case for the *value* of art in human life. Let us consider then the way the arts might enhance human understanding.

Art and Cognition

> There is more to the life of the human mind than conceptual thought; the activity of the senses is as much mental as that of intellectual reflection.[10]

Gordon Graham identifies two fundamental inquires in philosophical aesthetics: definitions of art and evaluative theories of its "social importance (or lack of it)."[11] Graham critiques the tradition of philosophical aesthetics as being too overly focused on the first of these, and suggests that a reverse of order might prove a more fruitful approach to the matter. Graham surveys the tradition of aesthetics, especially since Kant, and concludes that the search for an "essential 'Form' or universal 'Idea' called 'Art'" ends in inevitable frustration. He recommends, then, the construction of a normative theory of art that would facilitate the distinction of "art" from "non-art" and provide a way—simultaneously—of locating the relative value of art in a spectrum of values. For Graham, it is the cognitive value of art that represents its culminating value, and his argument for this position is worth considering.[12]

In an article published in 1995 entitled "Learning from Art," later incorporated into and expanded in his book *Philosophy of the Arts*, Graham argues for what he describes as a normative account of aesthetic cognitivism, as opposed to a descriptive one (i.e., an account of necessary and sufficient conditions of what can be considered art). Based on Nelson Goodman's account of how the arts pertain to the dynamic of "worldmaking," Graham argues that art can advance understanding, and does so primarily in two ways: by

10. Graham, *Philosophy of the Arts*, 3rd ed., 64.

11. Ibid., 3.

12. Ibid., 243–44.

directing the mind through progressions of thought and through expanded venues of perception of human experience.[13]

Graham's article begins as a response to an earlier article by Douglas Morgan, who argued against cognitive theories of art on the basis that such theories traffic in false alternatives between (a) art as mere diversion and decoration and (b) empirical knowledge, and the implied superiority of such a "scientific" understanding of knowledge against which art is then held. Graham acknowledges the rightness of resisting such reductionistic views of art, but argues that Morgan himself engages in a form of reductionism. According to Graham, Morgan's account of the cognitive potential of art is weakened by his equation of cognitive significance with propositional truth subject to falsification. Graham suggests that with the substitution of "truth" with "understanding," a new way of perceiving the cognitive dimension of the arts is available:

> Now while it may be true that works of art, even works of literature, do not direct abstract thought, it may none the less be true that they direct the mind, that is, direct the perception of the audience.[14]

All art moves the thought and attention of the reader or audience in certain ways: music through melodic and harmonic progressions; film through sequential images; paintings through visual cues such as foregrounding, points and convergence, color

---

13. Graham, "Learning from Art," 26–37. Graham makes reference to Goodman's *Ways of Worldmaking*.

14. Ibid., 32. In *Philosophy of the Arts*, Graham continues this line of thought:

> In this sense we can speak of works of art "directing the mind." They do not do this by constructing proofs and assembling evidence or even the presentation of propositional truths, but there are many examples of the other ways in which they do it. Rhythm in poetry, for instance, is more than a linguistic counterpart to music. By determining how we hear the line, and where the emphasis falls, rhythm can determine what the sense is. Composers, conductors, and performers all determine how music is heard, which sound predominates over others both acoustically and harmonically. Architects determine the order in which shapes and materials are seen by those who walk through the buildings they construct. And so on. (65).

and shading. All forms of art have their toolbox of techniques and conventions—their mode of rhetoric, if you will—through which they convey the thought and influence (though not determine) the perspective of the audience and move them toward implicit moral postures in relation to the subject matter of the artwork.

Graham also considers the knotty matter of the relationship between art and "reality." For previous theorists, art failed to, or no longer was interested in, the representation of reality and so art must be evaluated on other bases, such as the expression of emotion, the primary theory of art of the nineteenth and early twentieth centuries. But Graham suggests that such theories over-look something about the relationship between art and "reality" and proposes that, rather than assuming a movement from reality to art and assessing an artwork on that basis, instead, one begins with art and moves toward corresponding reality. Graham writes:

> To see how art can be a form of understanding, it is essential to grasp that it involves moving from art to experience, not from experience to art. It is true that the images by which we are confronted in art are always images of particulars, but as Aristotle points out in the case of drama, images and characters can be generalized. Bruegel's celebrated picture can be of a country wedding, and need not be of any particular country wedding. It will not alter its subject to discover that the faces and objects collected in it were never assembled together at any one time, or even that they ever never existed. Art may be imaginary through and through, but it can still enable us to look more sensitively at the people, circumstances and relationships in our own experience. The question to be asked of such a work is not, "Does this effectively capture the scene portrayed?" but *"Does this make us see this sort of occasion differently?"*[15]

One thinks, for example, of Francis Schaeffer's experience with Rembrandt's *The Slaughtered Ox* and how he claimed he could never see beef in a butcher shop in quiet the same way after encountering Rembrandt's painting. Now I would argue that

15. Graham, "Learning from Art," 35. Emphasis added.

normally and unselfconsciously we move in an oscillation from art to reality and back again in corresponding movements of discovery and verification, in the long course of which a richer understanding of life is forged. Graham nonetheless articulates a persuasive case for the cognitive value of art. Arts address more than feelings. They address ideas, values, and perceptions. Connecting these to the realm of the spiritual involves the work of theological aesthetics. As this chapter progresses I will propose a *descriptive analysis* of art that aims at strengthening the kind of normative account that Graham develops of the value of art for human flourishing.

Theological Aesthetics

Whereas philosophical aesthetics provides conceptual clarity, as well as a history of thought regarding art, beauty, and aesthetic experience, theological (or religious) aesthetics provides conceptual clarification along with an intentional reflection on art in relation to God. The work of Frank Burch Brown is an example of one of the widest and most comprehensive advances in the field of theological or religious aesthetics in the past twenty years.[16] Brown's contribution to this project lies in the example of his own working definition of art. Brown stipulates that no definition can successfully encompass all one might wish to say about art, nor need it "*rule* out what it *leaves* out." For his own definition, Brown writes:

> For our purposes art can best be defined as any and all of the creative skills, informed practices, and primary products manifest in the making of publicly recognizable aesthetica.[17]

16. Brown, *Religious Aesthetics*, 20.

17. Ibid., 86. Brown further elucidates this definition:

We will consider a work of art to be anything that is at least partially artificial in origin, that reflects creativity, skill, or knowledge, and that in large measure is, or could be, something appreciated by a public attentive to aesthetic factors such as form and style, and responsive to aesthetic effects such as those we regard as intrinsically interesting, expressive, or beautiful (Ibid., 88).

Brown develops his theory of art, with reference to the philosopher Immanuel Kant, as enabling one to "think more" than concepts themselves can contain. He continues:

> Clearly we should add, however, that perhaps some art allows one not only to think more but also to feel more, and that in both of these ways together it manages to mean more, possibly even letting one be and become more.[18]

Brown's work emphasizes religious aesthetics within a recognizably Christian yet intentionally general theological framework. Jeremy Begbie, on the other hand, has pursued these questions from a more carefully defined neo-Barthian or, in his own words, a more christologically determined set of convictions.[19] Begbie seeks to situate the arts in such a way that they can be seen to illuminate the purposes of God in creation and redemption. His agenda is to set out what he and others of similar theological perspective call a more *relational* account of the world and God, which for Begbie finds sponsorship in the doctrines of the Trinity, the incarnation, and the Pauline affirmations of creation and redemption in Christ.[20] For Begbie, therefore, whatever else they incorporate, the arts must be viewed as "ineluctably acts of communication."[21] The form of communication that Begbie finds most apt in describing the dynamics of art is that of *metaphor*. Metaphors, of course, involve the combination of two naturally unrelated things in such a way as to illuminate in some way the referent object. Consider that beautiful passage from *Hamlet*:

18. Ibid., 92.

19. Begbie, *Voicing Creation's Praise*, 167.

20. Ibid., 179f. Begbie is among Protestant theologians who, in light of Karl Barth's work, prioritized special revelation and with it an emphasis on Trinitarian doctrine. One outcome of this was an emphasis on the perichoretic implications of classic Trinitarianism, translated in terms of relationality. See Shults, *Reforming Theological Anthropology: After the Philosophical Turn to Relationality* for one account of this process.

21. Begbie, *Voicing Creation's Praise*, 220.

> But look, the morn in russet mantle clad
> Walks o'er the dew of yon high eastward hill.

A morning, of course, is a phenomenon involving the rotation of a planet on its axis in orbit around a star. But in describing a dawn in terms of a person dressed in red outerwear walking toward the viewer on the condensation of a hill, Shakespeare provides a new way of considering the phenomenology of the experience of morning. This is the way art works. Even art in its most realistic form is never the actual thing portrayed. It is *artifice*. But in the hands of a master, artificiality becomes illuminative, and since it is the master's choice of *what* to illumine and *how* to do so, artifice becomes edifice, a potentially enduring statement about something deemed worthy of consideration. In the example above, it is a brief, concentrated consideration of the experience of dawn.

For Begbie, like Gordon Graham, who works out this theme in greater philosophical nuance, the arts largely direct the mind toward greater insight into the character of creation and its redemption. This holds great promise for the development of a practical theology of art. But how might it be taken further toward an account of spiritual formation? Here the contribution of Aidan Nichols serves as a helpful resource. A scholar widely known for his work in exegeting the theology of Hans Urs von Balthasar, Nichols makes frequent recourse to the philosophy of phenomenology. Phenomenology, a movement of the mid-twentieth century, represents the attempt to restore a sense of balance between the subjective and objective realms of human experience, and introduces ways of conceptualizing the "dialogue" between a subject and the object of consideration. Phenomenology provides a way of establishing the integrity of an artwork, for example, with its own meaningful "presence" apart from whatever interpretive understanding a viewer may wish to draw from (or impose upon) the object.[22]

22. Nichols writes:
It is fortunate, therefore, that the resurgence of a visionary art with teaching to offer in the modern epoch has coincided with the rise of a school of aesthetics which takes artistic experience seriously as *a unique form*

In his book *The Art of God Incarnate*, Nichols explores the dynamics of disclosure as it is found in the revelation of God through prophetic discourse, supremely in the incarnation, and then in iconography and, by way of extension, in the visual arts in general. Nichols defines art as the "embodiment of meaning in the sensuous order."[23] Employing the analogue of language, Nichols writes:

> The sensuous element is responsible for the artwork's peculiar plenitude and its uniquely imposing form of presence. It "speaks to" us or "strikes" us through the glory of the sensuous realm to which it belongs. . . . The "weight" of the sensuous, rendered communicative by the artist's creative talent, accounts for the ability of the artwork to take an initiative with us and to be experienced by us as a kind of address.[24]

As "embodiment[s] of meaning in the sensuous order," artworks, for Nichols, communicate through two essential means. The first of these is its participation in a system of iconology, "a pattern of images and motifs in an artist's work or in a wider artistic tradition," which Nichols describes as a "network of visual images [that form] in art a sign-system which is a kind of visual analogue to language."[25] By this Nichols means the use and manipulation of conventions that become transformed into a unique

---

of communication not to be reduced to some more general category less than itself. This "phenomenological" school works with the philosophical method of the same name whose keynote is the self-discipline of the knowing agent before the object. As Martin Heidegger, a pioneer of this method, wrote in his early *Being and Time*, the being in question must "be seen as existing in its own self-disclosure." This re-direction of interest towards the object conceived in its own autonomy of existence is the more welcome in aesthetics since a rampant subjectivism has reigned too long. (*The Art of God Incarnate*, 90. Emphasis added).

23. Ibid., 94.

24. Ibid., 93.

25. Ibid., 94. It is evident that Nichols' primary point of reference in his analysis of the arts is painting. While this focuses (and limits) the scope of his analysis, its applicability to other forms of art remains. All forms of art have their traditions and conventions that make up the "language" of the art form.

address. "Just as a particular poet will rely on certain established metaphorical transformations of the literal in speech, so too an artist in his iconology will presuppose a background of stylistic convention from which his own creative innovations stand out."[26] Nichols notes that such conventions rely on particular cultural inheritances and contexts. These dynamics will be explored in two particular cases in chapters 3 and 4.

The second means of communication is what Nichols calls the "affective quality" of art, its "expressive" dynamic which translates a unique point of view into an emotionally arresting experience. Nicholas suggests that rightly perceiving this point of view requires care and sensitivity on the part of the receiver.[27] In any case, we are now a long way off from John Carey's despairing view of art. There are ways of understanding art that is intellectually responsible and morally meaningful. Viewed as unique means of communication through the "languages" of form, organization, sonority, movement or performance, the arts are objects that can "speak" to us if we are open and willing to engage with them on their terms.

Dynamics of Aesthetic Communication

Meaningful and formative encounters with art inevitably involve processes of *interpretation*. In this regard, some recent developments in biblical hermeneutics offer ways of understanding the interplay between artists, their work, and their audiences. The forge out of which these new insights are drawn involve the interface between certain postmodernist approaches to textual interpretation and responses from more traditionalist Christian biblical theologies, to wit, the battle between some radically indeterminist accounts of textual "meaning" and strategies that seek to ground what might be called an "open determinacy" of textual meaning, a kind of critical realism of interpretation. One strategy for such an "openly determined" or "hermeneutically realist" approach to

26. Ibid., 94.
27. Ibid., 98.

Scripture (as well as ordinary human texts) is the traditionalist account of the existence of God as a communicative Being and of humans made in the image of this communicative Creator.

A prominent figure in this traditionalist camp of biblical hermeneutics is Kevin Vanhoozer. Vanhoozer articulates a hermeneutic of openly determinant meaning grounded in the existence of God as an intrinsically (within a Trinitarian theology) and extrinsically (within a prophetic disclosure framework) communicative Being. The possibility of meaningful and meaning-full human discourse finds its grounding in such theological convictions. By way of its very title, *Is There a Meaning in This Text?* Vanhoozer issues a salvo across the bow of certain strands of literary criticism and its attendant postulates concerning human discourse. What is significant for the developing thesis here is Vanhoozer's recourse to speech-act theory for an account of human being and human meaning-making. Vanhoozer traces the rise of speech-act theory in the work of J. L. Austin and in particular John Searle. Both are grounded in the Ordinary Language Philosophy that arose in British philosophical circles in the 1940s and 1950s. Austin analyzed communication in terms of *locution* (the utterance itself), *illocution* (its intention), and *perlocution* (what the speech-act achieves). For Vanhoozer, it was Austin's stipulation of the illocutionary dimension that highlights (a) the existence of a speaker/author, who (b) is not only a speaker but a *doer*. In terms of the arts, one might suggest that speech-act theory reveals not only a doer but a *speaker/communicator*.[28]

A further articulation of this "common sense hermeneutical realist" approach to biblical interpretation is taken up by one of Vanhoozer's protégés who is herself a musician as well as a theologian.[29] Jeannine Brown advances the same interpretive strategies that Vanhoozer and others argue for in her hermeneutical methodology. But it is in the course of some tangential comments that she provides grist for a theo-aesthetic mill. Like Vanhoozer, Brown argues for a hermeneutically realist reading of Scripture that is

28. Vanhoozer, *Is There a Meaning in This Text?*, 208–9.
29. Brown, *Scripture as Communication*, 75.

confident yet "modest" in its claim of access to "authorial intent" and acknowledges the "location," or lived context, of the reader, even as it resists a "radical contextualization" in which everything is the reader's context and the authors' intention is lost. In this regard, Brown reflects the work of others in suggesting the potential of narrative theology to interrogate the "locations" of authors, texts, and readers:

> One way of attending to the biblical story envisioned by the biblical authors is to focus on what has been called "the world projected by the text." In fact, we may speak of entering the world of the text as a way of allowing its normative story to shape us.[30]

Brown mirrors Vanhoozer in commending the deployment of speech-act theory, and provides a summary of its benefits for the interpretation of Scripture. Stated in my own words, one could say that Brown's analysis underscores the dynamics of *intentionality, interpersonality,* and *integrity* in the process of receiving and "reading" a text or other communicative acts. Speech-act theory suggests that with words humans do not merely say things, but *do* things, and that there is generally integrity behind what they say/do. Brown suggests the example of the wedding ceremony, where as celebrants make vows they effect a change in their relationship.[31] Drawing on Austin's notions of the illocutionary dimension of human utterance, Brown suggests that speech-act theory highlights the often overlooked performative aspects of Scripture. Written texts do not merely project information; *they inculcate dispositions and insinuate responses.* Secondly, speech-act theory for Brown, as for Vanhoozer, "reintroduces the author" into textual interpretation, albeit under a refined, modest appraisal of access to authorial intention. Thirdly, even as speech-act theory revives the notion of the author (or the artist) as a "responsible communicative agent,"[32] it underscores an ethic of dialogical encounter, with potential application for a hermeneutic of the arts:

30. Ibid., 46.

31. Ibid., 32.

32. Vanhoozer, *Is There a Meaning in This Text?*, 204.

My goal when participating in communication with a friend is not to master what is communicated, or the person communicating it for that matter. Instead, I want to really hear and thereby know the other person more fully. Analogously, our goal in textual interpretation involves, at its heart, listening in order to hear well. This listening is attentive to what is being communicated, without requiring the assurance that I can reach some sort of pure objectivity. Instead, listening seeks relationship.[33]

Drawing together features of phenomenology, speech-act theory, reader-response strategies, and narrative theology, Brown reaches an account of meaningful interaction with a text that again has implications for interaction with art in general:

Repeated interaction with a text—particularly with the awareness of one's own presuppositions, the otherness of the text, and the storied nature of the whole—can move one productively toward textual understanding. For [Martin] Heidegger, this is the nature of the hermeneutical process: its circle. We might even expand the image to talk about a hermeneutical spiral, which moves toward greater and greater understanding. Yet this movement toward understanding must never be conceived in absolute terms, as if we can attain the perfect reading and the close the book. "Every time one goes around the spiral the lenses of the telescope have altered, but every time there are still lenses." At its heart, the hermeneutical process is open-ended, never fully completed. Maybe this should not surprise us, since an interpersonal view of hermeneutics invite the analogy of relationship or friendship, whose goal is not completion for its own sake but continual longing to know and to be known.[34]

Several things are striking. It is common now in certain quarters that all aspects of human relationship are thought of as "texts," but this does have potential usefulness in considering artistic phenomena. By suggesting that art can be or needs to be "read" again

33. Brown, *Scripture as Communication*, 73–74.
34. Ibid., 74.

underscores the *cognitively significant* dimension of the arts. Such a perspective would address several of John Carey's criticisms of nonliterary arts. Moreover, the analogy underlines the intentionality that generally sponsors works of art, and reiterates the fact that all art originates from and is received within contexts. It also underlines the interpersonality of the encounter between artists and auditor, and can inform a "hermeneutic of trust" that the artist means what apparently the work is "doing."

Brown's articulation of the "relational" dimension of interpretation as analogous to an open-ended friendship is interesting. But it is in her move to "take seriously the communicative nature of all texts without embracing a simplistic one-size-fits-all method of textual interpretation," that Brown advances a suggestive approach to communication theory. Brown suggests that one think of communication taking place within a spectrum that accounts for differing genre and intention, a spectrum consisting of, on one end, *transmissive* forms and intentions, and on the other, *expressive* forms and intentions. Toward the transmissive are speech-acts mostly in the first person directed to intended audiences for specific purposes. Letter writing and scientific writing are examples. On the expressive end, the arts stand as prime examples of more open-ended, less determined forms of communication, but forms of communication nonetheless. The Bible, in this analysis, exists within a dialectical relationship of these two poles of communicative intention, and any accurate reading of the Bible must attend to when the dynamics of this spectrum is in play:

FIGURE 02

Communicative Spectrum of Intentionality Types

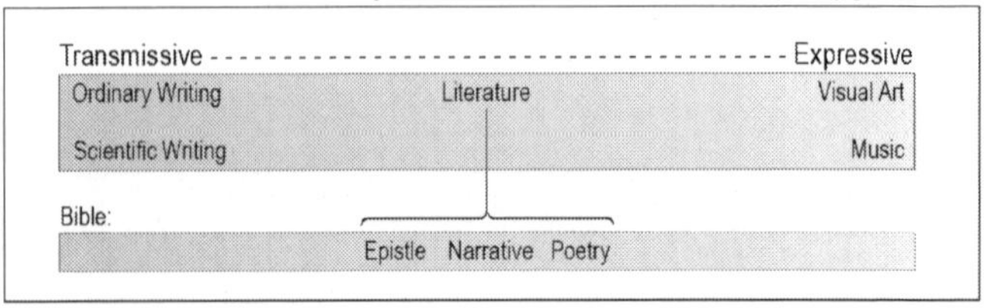

Transmissive - Expressive		
Ordinary Writing	Literature	Visual Art
Scientific Writing		Music
Bible:		
	Epistle Narrative Poetry	

Brown's diagram helpfully categorizes different acts of communication, as well as underlines the aesthetic dimension of Scripture, with the interpretive and experiential implications this suggests. It might be possible, however, to situate works of art at points all *across* this spectrum, rather than relegate it to just one side. Considering degrees of transmissive or expressive intentions might illuminate new aspects of a given piece. Most importantly, just as speech-act theory highlights that with words humans not only say things, but do things, likewise in art, human not only *do* things, but *say* things.

A Narrative Hermeneutic of Art

It is a commonplace to hear people reflect how a given work of art "spoke" to them. Contemporary artist Makoto Fujimura writes of his first encounter with the work of modernist artist Arshile Gorky:

> I remember going to the Arshile Gorky retrospective in the early eighties at the Guggenheim, and having the paintings *speak to me* in ways [Tōhaku Hasegawa's *Pine Forest*] *speaks to me* today. In fact, I believe that that experience convinced me that I should seek to pursue art. Gorky's works probed the depth of essentiation. Gorky's later works spoke in a *language* I could not comprehend but yet yearned for.[35]

If artistic expression, then, is analogous to language, how are these languages converted into unique forms of meaningful utterances?[36] I now begin to turn, then, toward a *descriptive account* of art—what art is—that I hope will clarify its ontology for the nonspecialist and increase its accessibility for the purpose of greater appreciation, enjoyment, and spiritual formation. Toward those purposes I argue that art is best understood as the

35. Fujimura, "That Final Dance," 300. Emphases added.

36. "Utterance" is used as a technical term within speech-act scholarship, frequently in relation to the nonverbal or language at its most embryonic.

employment of *craft*, the production of *content*, and the dynamics of *context*. Art is an amalgamation of craft, content, and context.

Art Involves Craft

> "It's a little insulting to craftsmen, skillful craftsmen . . ." he told Marr. "I used to point out at art school, you can teach craft, it's the poetry you can't teach. Now, they try to teach the poetry and not the craft."[37]

"Inspirational" notions of artistic activity fail to give due recognition to the reliance on conventions, the rhetorical strategies, and the years of practice, trial, and error that lie behind works of creativity. Recognizing the matter of craft rescues art from overprecious approaches and restores its vitality as forms of "made things." "Craft" is derived from the Greek *techné*, and refers to the actual process by which a "made thing" (one recognized definition of art) is produced. Craftsmanship, therefore, is a disciplined, acquired skill that requires practice and is generally subject to the appraisal of those who know the craft, namely the "guild."

In addition, art communicates in a particular way unique to a given craft, be that painting, music, sculpture, etc. Consequently, a large part of engaging with art is learning to understand the particular way an artwork is communicating, whether through rhythm and rhyme, melody and timbre, movement and gesture, line and color, or shape and form, etc. Craft involves the effective usage and manipulation of these means of communication.

Under the rubric of communication, craft in art refers to the learned and practiced deployment of skills and "grammar" to the end of meaningful communication. In this analysis, craft incorporates matters of "form" in as much as they occur as conventional means of *formulating* such skills and grammar in a given work.

37. David Hockney, speaking to Andrew Marr in an article reviewing recent downturns in the popularity of contemporary concept art, and particularly the work of Damien Hirst. Quoted in Smart, "Has Shock Art Lost Its Bite?," 16.

Normally art is considered the effective union of form and content, and this truism holds, but the effect of that union will be considered as part of its content. The successful deployment of formal means implies the existence of craft.

Highlighting the dimension of craft serves the following objectives:

1. Identifying craft as an essential dimension of art assists in establishing boundaries of what counts as art. Gordon Graham prefaces his analysis of art by identifying what makes art and what establishes its social value. His survey reveals that too little attention is given to the mere human excellence promoted by and attained in the pursuit of craft, and how its implication in the phenomenon of art would in itself validate the social value of art.[38] The arts are not indeterminate phenomena, but modes of practice and expression, constituted by craft and subject to the assessment and adjudication of a guild of practitioners.

2. Focusing on craft provides a means to engage with art on the level of skill and style. This is not to jettison emotional, visceral, or subjective responses to art, but to insist that art communicates something *in a particular way with particular skills* to an audience.

3. Emphasizing craft enables us to adjudicate between the decorative-functional and the expressive-communicative. A work of art may revel in decorative gestures, but this does not preclude the presence of communication. This distinction may be blurred, but in general *art "happens" when craft is transcended and a unique form of communication take place.*

4. Acknowledging the dimension of craft situates an artwork within a context of practice which constitutes part of the "story" within which it participates and thereby introduces to its audience. Noël Carroll argues that artworks are best "defined" according to the place they occupy within a genealogy

38. Graham, *Philosophy of the Arts*, 1–3.

of descent in a tradition of practice that can be articulated in narrative terms. This project opts for another line of definition, but Carroll's theory underlines the significance of the dimension of craft.[39]

5. Recognizing the role of learned craft provides a rationale for the existence of critical reviews of art and of a place for *informed opinion* about art, as opposed to mere personal preferences. This is why there is value in reading review articles on films, performances, concerts, and the like, as well as books and catalog articles from museums. Such materials can introduce us to aspects of the arts we might otherwise overlook, as well as help stretch our natural or received preferences and prejudices toward a greater scope of appreciation.

Art and Content

Content is that aspect of an artwork that recipients are generally first drawn toward, aware of, and wish to discuss. It is the text-music synthesis of song, the picture in a painting, the image created in a poem. Analysis of formal principles and organizing structures in a given artwork generally coincide with an analysis of what such principles and structures contain. Content in this light can be understood as *subject matter*. Given the almost inevitable use of conventions in any art form, content identifies what individuates a given example. If the *genre* of a painting (e.g., landscape) is considered a general aspect of its form, then content analysis might begin by identifying what the painting focuses the viewers' attention upon. Or the analysis might be much more specific, even down to the work of a single artist who nonetheless, though a practitioner of a particular form/style of painting, painted different things. Content is about what these different things were.[40]

39. Carroll, *Art in Three Dimensions*, 27f.

40. Wheaton College art historian E. John Walford advanced "content criticism" to redress an unbalanced concentration on formal properties in art. See Walford, *Jacob van Ruisdael and the Perception of Landscape*, and Romaine, ed., *Art as Spiritual Perception: Essays in Honor of E. John Walford*.

The thesis of this book is that not only the peculiar content of a particular piece, but the *gestalt* of the artistically handled form-content embodiment of a whole artistic oeuvre or of a cultural-historical location projects a perspective of life that issues in an invitation for the receiver to consider. I employ the term "story" in a multivalent manner, using it in reference at one point to the immediate import of a given work and sometimes to the larger and often implicit network of values, myths, and beliefs that guide artists in how they work in terms of craft and what they produce in terms of themes and subject matter. A Greek sculpts a female nude, a Zen Buddhist composes a minimalist haiku, a Muslim makes a calligraphic rendition of a Qur'anic verse. There is the content of the particular work and the "story," which it both participates in and expresses or "projects" as an act of communication.

Consider, for example, Beethoven's *Fifth Symphony*. The drive from tension to resolution inherited from the Western harmonic tradition carries within it a certain kind of teleology, a sense of moving forward in time toward an end. Beethoven takes this inheritance—the dramatic possibilities latent in forms like the sonata and the dramatic potential of moving from minor toward major key modality—and creates an even greater sense of momentum, from the conflict and hardship of the first movement toward the resolution and victory of the finale. Beethoven's symphonic "story" may be seen as culturally derivative from the Christian story with its themes of suffering and resurrection as distilled through Enlightenment progressivism. Beethoven's artistic narrative could be articulated as that of the victory of the human spirit over all obstacles. This implicit vision of life informs all of Beethoven's music. As it is often observed of preachers, Beethoven has his basic sermon of human achievement over all obstacles, preached with remarkable vitality, variety, industry, and inventiveness.

By identifying *story* as a basic feature of artistic phenomena, we affirm that art is both emotionally evocative and intellectually informative. In terms of intellectual gain, art introduces one to potentially new forms of *language* through which meaningful utterance can be made. As Gordon Graham argues, it provides opportunities for new *understanding* as a type of cognitive gain.

And the arts provide ways in which ideas can take affective hold and alter one's sense of value. As John Carey himself put it, "Because [poetic ideas] make you *feel as well as think*, you can appropriate them, grow into them, adopt them as your own."[41] I simply apply this dictum to all forms of art. Beethoven's Christian-Enlightenment anthem of revolutionary progress can shape or become one's own personal ethos. The music helps one think it as well as feel it.

Like any story, art engages the whole person, sometimes even eliciting a physical and moral response. To engage attentively to a Beethoven symphony may not only move a person emotionally, but may inspire him or her toward aspirational achievement in spite of adversity. Some religious believers may find this particular "story" a form of humanism they cannot endorse without qualification, but Beethoven's music at least makes this vision of reality profoundly plausible.

EXCURSUS

Ludwig van Beethoven (1770–1827)

Musicologist Scott Burnham expresses the confluence of ideological and cultural influences which both shaped and is given articulation in Beethoven's music:

> Fundamental to the worldview of the *Goethezeit* [Age of Goethe] is an ennobling and all-embracing concept of the self. The emerging

forms of romantic imagination" (to use M. H. Abram's expression) are based on the rhythms and scenarios of the individual self, such as birth and death, personal freedom and destiny, self-consciousness and self-overcoming. In Germany these currents swelled to create a new intellectual ethos, merging in an incipient cultural nationalism with the apotheosis of self, a merger instrumental in lending that nationalism the imprimatur of universality. Beethoven's heroic style has been heard not only to instantiate these values but to give them unimpeachable expression. [*Beethoven Hero*, 112–13].

41. Carey, *What Good Are the Arts?*, 246. Emphasis added.

Art in Context

Context here means everything it would mean in any typical art appreciation course. It includes the situatedness of the artwork within contexts of the artists' *oeuvre*, within schools of practice, and within a social and cultural *milieu*. It involves questions of how a work is implicated in the dynamics of its time, how it expresses "the deeper agenda of its age,"[42] and how it subsequently shapes the propagation, transmission, and reception of that meaning. Here, insights drawn from strands of postmodern literary and cultural criticism—art as "social discourse"—can be illuminating. While there are strands within this tradition that can be reductive or shrill in its analyses, postmodern analysis highlights and performs a necessary task: uncovering ways that the arts participate in the "stories" told by and within communities of human discourse. In this sense, arts are *artifacts* of particular places and times and of the "modes of discourse" within which it existed. Attending to matters related to context of origin provides means of access to better "hear" the story a given work of art is telling. This context is historical in as much as it involves time and place. It involves all those elements often alluded to under the catch-all notion of *worldview*. Seen from a certain perspective, arts are primary windows into worldviews; incarnations not only of values and the answers people give to questions, but the source of the *questions themselves*. Worldviews, in this sense, signal what is important to people and what they find worthy of questioning.

Artists do not create contexts; they work within them. Context is the web of complex circumstances in which artists work in relation to their physical environment, historical trends and traditions, social movements, cultural values, intellectual perspectives, personal commitments, and more. Art *originates* from within a context. Likewise, art is *received* within a context of corresponding dynamics that shape meaning and interpretation. As such, context is an inescapable dimension of art in both its production and its reception and interpretation. Recognizing the context of art—both

42. Burnham, *Beethoven Hero*, 142.

of its origin and reception— underlines the multivalent and open-ended character of interpretation. For example, the "meaning" of Beethoven's *Ninth Symphony*, the "Choral Symphony," with its text by Friedrich von Schiller, will vary depending on whether we are referring to its première in 1824, or when Wilhelm Furtwängler conducted it at a celebration of Hitler's birthday in Berlin in 1942, or when Leonard Bernstein conducted it before the newly opened Berlin Wall in 1989. Continuities and discontinuities of meaning abound, and a sensitive and informed engagement with a work of art will be cognizant of its originating context while continuing to interact with new meanings forged in ever-changing contexts of reception. Moreover, highlighting the context of art allows one to relate, when possible, aspects of authorial intent in dynamic interplay with other contextually relevant interpretations in our own communicative encounters with art.

All these considerations reflect the influence of postmodernist approaches to interpretation. Origin and reception analysis underline how, like artists themselves, works of art are not pristinely "innocent," but implicated in their worlds. This should inform any theological aesthetic and can certainly be seen as one dimension of a maturing relationship with the arts. The maturity involved in this level of sophistication becomes suggestive of the relationship between the arts and spiritual formation. Capacities for reflecting on the situatedness of art can in turn lead to similar reflections on the exegesis of Scripture as well as understanding and critiquing one's own style of worship and spirituality.

Conclusion

As stated above, my aim in this project is to stipulate an understanding of the arts that does justice to the complexity of the subject matter while rendering it accessible so that the catalytic potentials of the arts for spiritual formation might be better realized. The following, then, is a heuristic model, heurism referring to a process whereby something of complexity is simplified for the purposes of analysis or teaching. For such heuristic purposes the analysis of art outlined above can be modeled in the following manner:

FIGURE 03

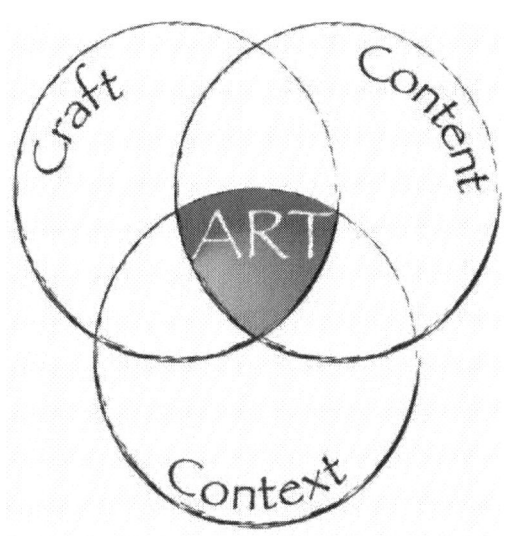

As diagrammed here, art is a complex phenomenon, an amalgamation, as I suggested earlier, of three analytically distinct but practically codependent dimensions without which art, as I understand it, does not exist.

As relatively stable but multivalent examples of human utterance, artworks can be experienced and "read" in such a way that meaning can be further accessed and its effect upon the receiver enhanced. Such a reading or exegesis of an artwork is best pursued along the lines of inductive reasoning, moving from the particular toward the general, avoiding the imposition of a meaning before the particulars of the work are allowed their full impact. Situating a given work within the body of an artist's output or an historic school can then serve as a guide or corrective against anachronistic or unduly idiosyncratic interpretations.

While an emphasis on processes of intellection may seem highlighted, the meaningfulness yielded in such a process often leads to enhanced personal meaningfulness. And while affirming the communicative functions of the arts, this is not at all to suggest the reduction of artworks to detachable "messages." What is being affirmed here is that the intuition that a work of art or a performance "spoke" to an audience is an accurate one if understood in a nuanced manner that respects the irreducibly embodied nature of aesthetic utterance. Artworks are windows into worldviews, means of storytelling that invite the receiver into these projected worlds, and provide a means of vicariously "trying them out." As such, engagement with the arts entails a measure of risk; "indwelling" an artist's work can be likened to entering their home, the sphere of their unique influence. The effects cannot—and should not—be predetermined.

While this chapter has emphasized the cognitive and communicative dynamics of art, this project concerns itself with an account of how the arts foment spiritual formation. Christian spirituality, however, involves more than just the vague enhancement of personal interiority. It involves moral formation, personal maturation, and an expanded capacity to respond to religious matters; to have "ears that hear and eyes that see" in such a way as to be pliable for transformation and service.

3

Aesthesis, Ascesis, and Catalysis

> Go to the pine if you want to learn about the pine, or to
> the bamboo if you want to learn about the bamboo. And
> in doing so, you must leave your subjective preoccupa-
> tion with yourself. Otherwise you impose yourself on the
> object and do not learn.[1]

It is the purpose of this book to explore the relationship between
the arts and spiritual formation. In my doctoral dissertation I articulated the relationship between the arts and spirituality in terms
of *aesthesis* or sensory perception (sense) and *ascesis* or disciplined
activity (spirituality) aimed toward progressive spiritual growth,
mediated and facilitated by art as *catalysis*. The question now is,
how might art catalyze such a relationship?

The Bewildering Minute

In his published and private prose writings, T. S. Eliot ruminated
on literary criticism, the meaning of the term "classic," and groped
toward a program of cultural recovery, which he felt the Western
world desperately needed. In a letter to literary critic Stephen
Spender, Eliot outlined what he believed to characterize the

---

1. Matsuo Bashō, quoted in Yuasa, "Introduction" in Bashō, *The Narrow
Road to the Deep North and Other Travel Sketches*, 33.

necessary experience required to critique a work with authenticity and insight:

> You don't really criticize any author to whom you have never surrendered yourself. . . . Even just the bewildering minute counts; you have to give yourself up, and then recover yourself, and the third moment is having something to say, before you have wholly forgotten both surrender and recovery. Of course the self recovered is never the same as the self before it was given.[2]

This three-step progression of surrender, recovery, and transformative integration is highly suggestive for theological aesthetics. Surrender suggests an opening of one's self to the potential impact of a work of art, to its influence and insinuations. It is to become vulnerable to its potential challenge. Eliot elaborates on this notion of surrender when he writes:

> The experience of a poem is the experience both of a moment and of a lifetime. It is very much like our intenser experiences of other human beings. There is a first, or an early moment which is unique, of shock and surprise, even of terror . . . a moment which can never be forgotten, but which is never repeated integrally; and yet which would become destitute of significance if it did not survive in a larger whole of experience; which survives inside a deeper and a calmer feeling.[3]

This kind of openness, this surrender, marks a clear point of confluence between the aesthetic and the spiritual, as those who know recognize that no significant religious or spiritual change takes place without a moment, and a general posture, of surrender

---

2. Allen Tate, "Remembering Eliot," in *T. S. Eliot: The Man and his Work*, edited by Allen Tate, quoted in Kermode, "Introduction," in *Selected Prose of T. S. Eliot*, edited by Kermode, 17. C. S. Lewis expresses a very similar perspective when he writes: "The first demand any work of any art makes upon us is surrender. Look. Listen. Receive. Get yourself out of the way. (There is no good asking first whether the work before you deserves such a surrender, for until you have surrendered you cannot possibly find out)." (Lewis, *An Experiment in Criticism*, 19.)

3. Eliot, "Dante," in *Selected Prose of T. S. Eliot*, edited by Kermode, 216.

to the divine presence. Capacity for surrender in one sphere may well assist such a capacity in the other.

Equally important for Eliot, however, are the stages of recovery and integration, of placing the drama of the initial encounter within the "larger whole" of one's experience of life. This is suggestive of the cumulative effect of encounters with the arts as well as of significant religious experiences. There is within this oscillation of tension and recovery the implication of growth, strengthening, resilience, and maturation.

Eliot's description of the experience of new discovery and integration in relation to the arts also underscores another important dynamic of art and spirituality, that of the dialogical character of sense and spirituality. David Brown's work frequently highlights this phenomenon. Brown's work advances a greater degree of dialogue between one's convictions and a work of art, which does not require the abandonment of conviction, but the suspension of judgment before a full encounter is made. Reflecting on the otherwise magisterial work of two major twentieth-century theologians for whom the aesthetic was significant, Hans Urs von Balthasar and Karl Barth, Brown writes of "little sense of learning or of discovery, and more a feeling of the imposition of predetermined judgments."[4] Aidan Nichol's deployment of a phenomenological approach takes a similar turn. Sensitivity to art requires what Nichols terms "appropriate dispositions." Nichols writes:

> To allow the artwork to speak we must not muffle it by a barrage of our own prior feelings, memories and mental habits. When on achieving this suspension of egoism we succeed in seeing the artwork in the pregnant aesthetic sense of "to see" we find that the feeling-quality of disinterestedness gives way to fresh and original feelings called forth by the artwork itself.[5]

Nichols continues:

4. Brown, *God and Enchantment of Place*, 7.

5. Nichols, *The Art of God Incarnate*, 98.

> Art requires and releases an *askesis* or discipline of vision
> so that we learn how to look with a purity of insight into
> the heart of human life. Such looking shifts our whole
> way of reading the significance of the world. In its wake
> we find our own existence reshaped from the experience
> of what we have seen.[6]

"Such looking shifts our whole way of reading the significance of the world." What Nichols describes here is a movement from looking to significance, and from apprehensions of significance back to looking even more. This is the mutually enriching, dialectically informing dynamic of sensory perception and practice, which matures and deepens over time, and which results in shifting (and presumably enriching) developments in the experience and perception of the significance of things.

Consider how this applies to one's experience with reading the Bible. Passages one has read for years and years, heard preached on for years and years, suddenly take on new significance. Perhaps this is due to hearing it in a new context, or a different translation, or presented within a different theological framework. But reading or absorbing the Word of God requires an open mindedness, an attitude that you haven't heard it all before, putting aside as best one can the barrage of "prior feelings, memories and mental habits."

The same dynamics then apply to art. What if Francis Schaeffer, for example, had pressed just a little further in his longtime admiration for Rembrandt's *Slaughtered Ox*? He no longer looked at hanging beef the same way. But did he not see the cruciform image of the flayed ox? And if such an identity with the crucified Christ was intended, then what of the implications of so associating the crucified Jesus with meat? After all, how does on attain full communion with the humanity of the Risen Lord if not by eating his flesh? Might there be, in the understated Dutch Protestant visual language of Rembrandt, a eucharistic suggestion in the painting? Perhaps Schaeffer did see this, but if so it would have involved his putting aside the "mental habits" born of his

---

6. Ibid., 100.

conservative Reformed theology toward a more sacramental way of understanding the significance of such a painting.

Reinstating the Spirit

Eliot's reflections on aesthetic *knowing* remain suggestive and brief, and focused primarily on developing capacities for poetic production and literary criticism. A far more developed account of creative epistemology to which several generations of religious thinkers have drawn upon is that of the chemist and philosopher of science Michael Polanyi (1891–1976). Polanyi advanced a species of epistemic critical realism focused less on the theoretical justification of knowledge as on the dynamics of the discovery and integration of knowledge. Polanyi reinstated a personalist dimension of knowledge which contrasted with the kind of positivism that dominated much of the twentieth century. As one contemporary Christian philosopher writes in a Polanyian mode, "All knowing is the profoundly human struggle to rely on clues to focus on a pattern that we then submit to as a token of reality." It is this human struggle (reliant upon what Polanyi calls "subsidiary" or tacit knowing) toward the apparent or emerging pattern (the "focal" dimension of the discovery process) that constitutes growth in knowledge. Such an account of knowledge results neither in epistemic despair nor absolute certainty, but a reliability subject to revision and reassessment.[7]

One concept that Polanyi made use of and has been picked up on by many subsequent theologians is that of "indwelling." This refers to the way we see through our already existing epistemic assumptions and instincts, but which assumptions and instincts can be altered, even radically altered, with new discoveries and insights. We focus upon the *focal* through our *subsidiary* knowledge, assumptions and instincts—our worldview if you will—but when focal discoveries are made then our subsidiary structures are changed.[8]

7. Meek, *Loving to Know: Covenant Epistemology*, 67–69.

8. Ibid., 458–61.

All of this is helpful in an intellectual sense. What of the spiritual? Here the work of the late James Loder offers a fruitful way of taking these suggestions toward a more thoroughly theological manner of thinking and application.

Before his death in 2001, Loder was the Professor of the Philosophy of Christian Education at Princeton. Central to Loder's thought was his use of the concept of "spirit." Loder's theological and anthropological pneumatology is that "the human spirit is to humanity what the Holy Spirit is to God (1 Corinthians 2:10)," namely the means of transformative self-awareness and self-expression.[9] *Spirit* for Loder meant both the Third Person of the divine Trinity and the dynamic of potential change and transformation of the human person. The Spirit of God related the transcendent God to human experience and the spirit in human existence opened humans to fresh discoveries about themselves and of God. It was Loder's professional mission to reinstate the presence of human spirit and the Holy Spirit back into human development theory and Christian education, grounded in what he called an "irreducibly spiritual" account of human learning, discovery, and maturation.[10]

9. Loder, *The Logic of the Spirit: Human Development in Theological Perspective*, 35.

10. See also Haitch, "A Summary of James E. Loder's Theory of Christian Education," in Wright and Kuentzel, eds., *Redemptive Transformation in Practical Theology*. Haitch, one of Loder's last doctoral students, articulates his teacher's understanding of spirit in a manner relevant to this study:

What, then, is "spirit"? The human spirit is best characterized as *creativity*. In his survey of the human spirit in Western thought, G. Thomas finds that the spirit has been equated with reason, love, (particularly eros), personality, universality, freedom, and creativity. Loder chooses the last as the mode that includes the others and more. If we press further to ask, But what is creativity? Then I think we must come to Loder's emphasis on *relationality*. Human creativity resides in the spirit's inherent relationality. We are not only egocentric, self-relating, but also exocentric, relating to what is beyond us. Thus, in *The Logic of the Spirit*, Loder suggests that "human spirit" is well characterized as "openness to the world and self-transcendence." Meanwhile in *The Knight's Move*, he says ("with a debt of gratitude to W. Pannenberg") that the human spirit is "a dynamic tension between 'centeredness' and 'openness.'" To define the spirit in words may be like trying to catch the wind in a net, so let the present congeries suffice: the human spirit has or

Loder's work drew on a number of sources in theology, the human sciences, the physical sciences, and the arts, resulting in an eclectic methodology. While appreciative of epigenetic accounts of "religious development" in age-related stages of occurrence, Loder sought a more existential account that drew on experiences of significant change involving both human choice and divine initiative. It was his analysis of such "crisis" experiences of change and the "transformation" of understanding that both informed Loder's theology of the spiritual and motivated his work to reinvigorate the analysis of the spiritual in contemporary theory of human development and religious education.

What is important for our purposes is his proposal of a sequence of transitional steps or stages that comprise what he called "convictional knowing," that is, decisive discoveries that change a person's understanding of themselves, of God and of the world, change as Loder would put it that "reopened the question of reality." His reliance upon Polanyi's work is clear, even as he takes it in new directions.

Drawing strongly upon episodes of profound theoretical change in scientific procedure and theory, as well as encounters with and the production of art, Loder outlined this (not necessarily linear) sequence of steps of transformative discovery as involving: (1) a conflict, that is, some sort of challenge to what had been normal perspective, belief, assumption about this. Such conflict may occur in contexts as different as the beginning of addiction recovery, school homework, Bible study, scientific research, or an encounter with a different or disturbing work of art. If the challenge of the conflict is accepted rather than avoided, then comes what Loder calls (2) an "interlude for scanning" or in the more Polanyian phrase the *indwelling* of the problem aided (or hindered) by subsidiary resources, resolved by (3) a constructive act of the imagination, that is, an insightful or intuitive response or solution

is creativity, relationality, exocentricity, openness, self-transcendence. Now the further take-away idea here is that humanity, spirit, and transformation go together. The dynamics of transformation point to spirit, and spirit points back to the fact that transformation is even more definitive of what it means to be human than is socialization (ibid., 306–7).

to the perceived conflict, (4) the nearly simultaneous release of the pent-up energy of the research, concentration or mulling of the problem, concluding with (5) a placement of the new insight back into the previous perception of things that both (potentially) changes that perception and integrates the new insight into a larger whole. This, of course, recalls what Eliot refers to as the recovery and the integration of the experience back into "a larger whole of experience" that, in Loder's terminology, now constitutes a new convictional knowing "inside a deeper and a calmer feeling." Such can be the process of a spiritual conversion, or of the spiritual formation that can occur when we allow, for example, a work of art to have its way with us, reopening for us questions of reality.

For Loder, the initiating "problem" which creates a kind of crisis will yield new knowledge or insight only to the degree that one cares about the challenge.[11] The arts can instantiate such challenges. An unfamiliar, jarring image of Christ. The stipulation of God's presence in an otherwise profane context. A slow-moving, meandering piece of music that seems to be going nowhere. Such might be the initial impressions of a work of art and may remain simply that unless the invitation or the challenge of the piece is taken up. Casual encounters with art—as with people or as with God—rarely yield new knowledge or transformative insight. The "cognitive dissonance" that some works of art create may increase our initial desire to avoid or move on from them. But with some suspension of judgment and "surrender," however tentative, to the artworks, such pieces hold at least the potential of new insight. Subsidiary knowledge—the assumptions and instincts by which things were previously interrogated—undergo alteration in preparation for new challenges on which to apply focal attention.

Loder's understanding of the relationship between sense and spirituality is perhaps best captured in his reflections on transformation in relation to the aesthetic, which for him involved the potential to . . .

---

11. Loder, *The Transforming Moment*, 36

break the numbing spell of "everydayness," to renew and restore both the human spirit and the particulars of the world. Dynamically, the human spirit, whether it be the artist's or the audience's, is characterized by its power to break with the tyranny of the obvious and compose some aspect of the world, in its (the spirit's) own terms.[12]

Looking and Looking

My own account of the relationship between sense and spirituality seeks to center on art as a catalyzing mediator for the relationship between sense and spirituality which provides opportunities for the development of eyes that see and ears that hear, to employ the biblical metaphor, or what we might refer as an increased capacities to accommodate truths about God and to participate in what His Spirit is doing in the world.

The heuristic model of the composite nature of the arts attempts to explain the arts along the lines of what I call a realistic ontology. Art involves the deployment of learned crafts that communicate perspectives on life shared explicitly by the artist or reflected implicitly in ways perhaps not recognized by the artists or performers themselves. The model seeks to enshrine both the uniqueness of art while demystifying it.

I advocate an approach to the arts that follows inductive reasoning, moving from particular toward more general conclusions and perspectives. I commend James Loder's five-step outline as one such approach, and particularly re-commend his suggestions regarding the engagement with conflict and the mode of indwelling the conflict as a form of contemplative attentiveness. I recommend allowing the artwork to have its "say" before the imposition of secondary commentaries is considered, and that inductive reasoning generally best serves to safeguard one's sense of the self-revealing potential of the piece under consideration.

Apart from these considerations, I proffer a series of values that I think underscore the general thesis of this project, namely

12. Ibid., 51–52.

that the dynamics of sensory perception and spiritual formation can act dialectically to the development of increased capacities for both spheres. First, the arts engender dispositions of attentiveness. In the literature of spirituality one doesn't read far before encountering the name of Simone Weil. In her later writings, Weil stipulates the importance of attentiveness and that it "consists of suspending our thought, leaving it detached, empty and ready to be penetrated by the object."[13] Drawing on the contemplative tradition, beginning in Plato and continued through Christianity, Weil argued that attentiveness is analogous to prayer, indeed it is an act of prayer itself because in such attentiveness there is a trust in the implicit presence of God in the object of one's attention.[14] Here one is reminded also of David Brown's suggestion of God sacramentally extending His presence through encounters with art. It does not require an elaborate account of divine presence in art to maintain that the act of practicing attentiveness, of "looking and looking," as Francis Schaeffer said, can lead to spiritually beneficent experiences with the arts. The arts invite, indeed almost require, that we slow down, wait, listen, defer judgment, achieve a "suspension of egoism," as Aidan Nichols writes, in order to break into "fresh and original feelings called forth by the artwork itself."[15]

Secondly, related to the value of attentiveness is this notion of indwelling. The capacity to see things through the lens of a work of art, to, however momentarily, take on its "affective quality" and appreciate its point of view, enables us to enter into other worlds, including that of the Bible, which in its premodern historical context is a very different world to ours.

Thirdly, artworks widen the sphere of our awareness and awaken imaginative possibilities. Many Christians rightly take encouragement from the recent popularity of film adaptations of books by C. S. Lewis and J. R. R. Tolkien. Some see similar

13. Miles, "Introduction," in Weil, *An Anthology*, 8.

14. Weil, "Attention and Will," in Weil, *An Anthology*, 231–37. Leighton Ford has treated this subject for a general readership in *The Attentive Life: Discerning God's Presence in All Things*, which includes a chapter on Simone Weil.

15. Nichols, *The Art of God Incarnate*, 98.

potentials even in the celebrated Harry Potter series, for these films all share in compelling presentations of themes of transcendence, sacrifice, redemption, faith, and resistance to irreducible evil. On the other hand, films such as *Children of Men*, *The Color of the Cross*, and *Jesus of Montreal* present traditional Christians with new ways of understanding the meaning of their beliefs and of how classical aspects of doctrine might be appropriated outside the bounds of traditional orthodoxy. When artworks of abstraction or challenging conceptualization are considered, then even more can Christians see the world in different ways, much as when a non-Christian first encounters the world of Scripture or the teachings of Christian faith. This can be disorienting or even threatening at times, but one might recall the new "poetry" that the biblical prophets introduced to God's people, or the jarring truths told slant in Jesus' parables.

Related to this proposition is that, fourthly, encounters with art help us see that formal structures are not only conveyors of insight, but are constitutive aspects of the insight. Biblical poetry, or prophetic oracle, or proverbial aphorisms, to name a few, are not merely means of revelation, but integral *aspects of* revelation. An incarnational faith such as Christianity does not consider the humanity of Jesus, even his very body, in a merely instrumental manner. His body is intrinsic to the revelation of his person and purpose. What an artist chooses as their formal vehicle, that is, the conventional structures and patterns they choose to employ, becomes constitutive of not only *how* they want to communicate, but *what* they want to communicate. The parables are not just a way of making complicated ideas easier to comprehend. They constitute something of the very truth of the gospel. The gospel is parabolic in nature. The examples from biblical studies could be multiplied. The point that I hope is being suggested is that there is an inescapably aesthetic dimension—a dimension involving sensory reception and perception—to revelation that is related in a principled way to the dynamics of God's working, especially in the incarnation.

One important and final insight that theological aesthetics illuminates is that of the relationship between style and substance. Much has been written recently on the arts and worship and liturgy.[16] It is often stated, for principled and irenic reasons, that while there are a variety of styles, there remains a unified substance of Christian doctrine. While there is truth in this observation, it requires some qualification. Within a theological aesthetics analysis, style and substance, like form and content, can be differentiated, *yet remain vitally connected.* The relationship between *aesthesis* and *ascesis* is perhaps nowhere more apparent than in the regular experiences of worship. Highly structured or highly improvisatory, celebrative or somber, iconic, aniconic, hymns, chants, choruses, or mixed variety, all of these and more conspire to explicitly or implicitly communicate truth-claims about the divine.

16. See for example Benson, *Liturgy as a Way of Life.* See also Dyrness, *Senses of the Soul.*

Excursus

James E. Loder (1931–2001)

Loder held the chair of the Philosophy of Christian Education at Princeton Theological Seminary for nearly twenty years. His passion was advancing an understanding of "convictional knowing" that not only informed but transformed the person and brought them closer to the existential realities of life. Loder summarized his outline of the "transforming moment" of spiritual change as follows:

> The transformational dynamic begins in conflict, moves through a *scanning* phase, comes up with an *insight* that resolves the conflict, and *releases the energy* bound up with it in a "Eureka!" *repatterning* of the self-world relationality and *proving* out the adequacy of the resolution. This dynamic combines continuity with discontinuity in what Michael Polanyi calls the most fundamental form of knowing: the act of discovery in the sciences, the act of creation in the arts—both powerful expressions of the human spirit. [*The Logic of the Spirit*, 113].

Loder would also affirm that along with discovery and creation lie interpretive breakthroughs such as can be occasioned in encounters with the arts, especially artworks that are challenging and perhaps difficult.

Part II

Practical Application

Introduction

The intention of this section is to apply in a more concrete manner the proposals and suggestions of the foregoing section. What does it look like to consider a work of art in terms of its craft, content, and context, to consider its story, and what may be the implications for such an analysis for spiritual formation?

Although I maintain that there are spiritually formative potentials in all manner of art projecting all manner of worldviews, not just specifically religious art, I have chosen three works ranging from poetry, painting, and music from confessionally Christian artists. I do so because of my own familiarity with these works and artists, because I believe they are worthy of attention, and because they are easily poised for a consideration of spiritual formation. The works themselves I believe are so inherently significant that I am freed from making only the most general of suggestions regarding their spiritually formative potential. One is from a deceased and celebrated artist, although I feel the work I focus on is too often overshadowed by earlier work and deserves renewed consideration in our day. The other two are living artists who are still in the midst of productive careers. One has gained a certain cache in American Evangelical circles; the other is hardly known at all in the United States, but has a considerable presence in the artistic life of Great Britain. My analysis of each of these works will proceed along the terms of my analysis of artworks as products involving craft, content, and context. The order of these dimensions is not important, although I will begin each chapter with a consideration of craft, as I believe this involves the fundamental "language" of the given artwork.

Some who are experienced with or have expertise in the arts of poetry, painting, or music may find my account of craft and technique lacking in detail or insufficiently developed. I do not wish to write full-blown commentaries on these works, but something more akin to liner notes for a record album. My aim is to provide the non-expert an introduction to the craft, to aspects of its means of communication, and how the particular artist inherited and advanced the medium in their works. It is my hope to provide a wide audience a way of beginning or advancing along the path toward the kind of *informed opinion* that I believe can only be gained from exposure and experience with a given art form.

As I suggest above, I decline to press too deeply or specifically in the spiritually formative potential of these works. I feel that the analysis will speak for itself of how these works might catalyze the relationship between sense and spirituality. Moreover, it is my fondest hope that my analyses, such as they are, will move readers to engage with the works themselves. That would be the most spiritually formative thing I can do for those who have followed along thus far. So I offer no wholesale explanations of any of these works. I seek only to set them before my readers for their consideration and further exploration, and to explicate aspects of their aesthetic ontology, which I identify as their craft, content, and context.

4

T. S. Eliot: *Four Quartets*

> What the poems do require is a trained ear, or at least the
> willingness to be trained.[1]

The words above are T. S. Eliot's reflections on the poetry of
his erstwhile friend and editor, the American poet Ezra Pound
(1885–1972). Like Pound, Thomas Stearns Eliot (1888–1965) was
born in the United States, but made England his permanent home
and nationality (Pound moved on to live in Italy after a long stay
in England). Eliot was a prolific writer of prose essays, treatises,
and literary criticism, a playwright, a journal editor, and a poet.
He is most immediately identified with his 1922 poem *The Waste
Land*. His set of poems entitled *Old Possum's Book of Practical
Cats* (1939) is the basis of the popular musical "Cats," and fans
of Francis Ford Coppola's films are familiar with Marlon Brando's
brooding recitation of *The Hollow Men* (1925) in the 1979 film
Apocalypse Now. His final major work of verse is a collection of
four poems whose compositions date from 1935 through 1942
that were drawn together to form *Four Quartets*. Fragments of the
poems have become part of our cultural cliché: "In my beginning
is my end"; "Fare forward, travelers"; ". . . you are the music/While
the music lasts"; "We shall not cease from exploration/And the end
of all our exploring/Will be to arrive where we started/And know

---

1. Eliot, "Ezra Pound: His Metric and Poetry," in *Selected Prose of T. S. Eliot*,
edited by Frank Kermode, 150.

the place for the first time." Like phrases from *Hamlet* they are easily recognizable, but the work from which they are drawn is not as well known.

Craft

As a poet, Eliot is usually placed among the forebearers and progenitors of literary modernism. His poetry reflects many of the techniques and preoccupations of English language poetry between 1905 and 1945, such as economy of expression, rhythmic vitality, topical relevancy, and the like. His presence was strong enough to elicit countervailing moves from other noted poets, including e. e. cummings, William Carlos Williams, and Allen Ginsburg. Eliot was a mountain one either climbed on or jumped off of.

In his prose writings Eliot expressed concern that since the seventeenth century Western culture had experienced a "dissociation of sensibility," by which he meant a breaking down of a coherent system of thought, belief, and polity, along with the tastes and judgments commensurate with such a civilization. One might say that "sensibility" represents for Eliot that union of sense and spirituality which is the hallmark of a mature culture. According to Eliot, poets after the seventeenth century could no longer "feel their thought" as could a John Donne or a George Herbert.[2] In one essay Eliot speaks of a literary separation of wit and magniloquence, that is, of sharp insight into the human condition rendered in language of appropriate expression.[3] From the seventeenth century onwards poets, in Eliot's estimation, become more self-conscious and "reflective" in a secondary and less immediate manner. The sixteenth-century metaphysical poets, for Eliot, had their faults, "[b]ut they were, at their best, engaged in the task of trying to find the verbal equivalent for states of mind and feeling."[4]

2. Eliot, "The Metaphysical Poets," in *Selected Prose of T. S. Eliot*, edited by Frank Kermode, 64.

3. Eliot, "Andrew Marvell," in *Selected Prose of T. S. Eliot*, edited by Frank Kermode, 162.

4. Ibid., 65. For further discussion of "sensibility," see Lewis, *Studies in Words*, 159–61.

For poets like Eliot and Pound, English language poetry had to be modernized to make it adequate for the task of expressing the modern states of mind and feeling: "our concern was speech, and speech impelled us/To purify the dialect of the tribe/And urge the mind to aftersight and foresight."[5] John Milton, John Dryden, and the generation when, according to Eliot, the "dissociation" took hold were great poets, but no longer "explorers of the soul" as Donne, Herbert, and others had been. By "soul" Eliot meant the integrative center of human existence; not just the heart: "One must look into the cerebral cortex, the nervous system, and the digestive track."[6] Eliot was anti-Romantic in this sense.

Whether we agree with Eliot's estimations of earlier poets or his characterizations of them is not important. What is important is the light his criticism sheds on his approach to his craft and sense of mission. It was Eliot's intention to heal the "dissociation," to give the English language back to itself and to restore this integrative "sensibility." Eliot's means of advancing this project is no easy retrieval of earlier styles or safe sentiments. Modern conditions, for Eliot, imposed the requirement that poetry become more *difficult*:

> Our civilization comprehends great variety and complexity, and this variety and complexity, playing upon a refined sensibility, must produce various and complex results. The poet must become more and more comprehensive, more allusive, more indirect, in order to force, to dislocate if necessary, language into his meaning. . . . Hence we get something which looks very much like the conceit—we get, in fact, a method curiously similar to that of the "metaphysical poets," similar also in its use of obscure words and of simple phrasing.[7]

Obscure words and simple phrasing. Helen Gardner, still the best commentator on Eliot's poetry, proposed that Eliot's greatness

5. Eliot, "Little Gidding," in *Collected Poems: 1909–1962*, 205.

6. Eliot, "The Metaphysical Poets," in *Selected Prose of T. S. Eliot*, edited by Frank Kermode, 66.

7. Ibid., 65. By *conceit* Eliot means "the elaboration (contrasted with the condensation) of a figure of speech to the furthest stage to which ingenuity can carry it," which is characteristic of the style of the "metaphysical" poets (60).

lies most in his creation of an innovative and effective poetic meter, of which *Four Quartets* is the supreme expression.[8] Gardner
describes Eliot's effort to, as it were, reassociate sensibility, as tack-
ling the problem of how "the greatest thoughts can be expressed
naturally." She continues:

> If we can discover a poetic rhythm in the most com-
> monplace speech, this rhythm may then be capable of
> refinement and elevation so that it may accommodate
> the greatest thoughts without losing naturalness.[9]

It is this naturalness of expression matched with complexity
of thought that characterizes Eliot's poetry. On this basis Gardner
offers her own prescription for an effective encounter with his
work:

> It is better in reading poetry of this kind to trouble too
> little about the "meaning" than to trouble too much. If
> there are passages whose meaning seems elusive, where
> we feel we "are missing the point," we should read on,
> preferably aloud; for the music and the meaning arise at
> "a point of intersection," in the changes and movement
> of the whole. We must find meaning in the reading,
> rather than in any key which tells us what the rose or
> the yew-tree "stands for," or in any summary of systems
> of thought, whether Pre-Socratic or Christian. Reading
> in this way we may miss detailed significances, but the
> whole rhythm of the poems will not be lost, and gradu-
> ally the parts will become easier for us to understand.[10]

It is helpful, then, to have some understanding of what Eliot
is *doing* in his poetry and allow it to guide our experience of his
work. Eliot is singing, as it were, and catching on to the rhythms
and cadences of his song will open the way toward greater comprehension, rather than the other way around. And if, as is sometimes then case, after some half-forgotten but unsatisfying initial

8. Gardner, *The Art of T. S. Eliot*, 15. Gardner mentions Pre-Socratic
thought because Eliot, ever fond of epigraphs, introduces *Four Quartets* with
two Greek passages from the Pre-Socratic philosopher Heraclitus.

9. Ibid., 25.

10. Ibid., 54.

encounter with Eliot's work either in school or in some other context, curiosity and interest can be rekindled with an appreciation of the problems Eliot felt confronted the modern poet and of his approach to adequately respond to them.

EXCURSUS

Rhythm and Meter in Poetry

In the epigraph to this chapter, Eliot commends Pound's poetry as requiring a training of the ear. So accustomed are we to the *reading* of poetry that they may have thought Eliot should have spoken of training the eye. But poetry always was, and ideally remains, an aural phenomenon, meant to be heard, not silently read.

Rhythm and meter, which are musical terms, are central dimensions of poetic craft. Edward Hirsch describes the dimension of rhythm:

> The poem is a muscular and composed thing. It moves like a wave and hypnotizes words into phrases, phrases into lines, lines into stanzas. As readers we simultaneously produce and perceive poetic rhythm [*How to Read Poetry*, 306].

British actor, presenter, and author Stephen Fry writes with characteristic wit and verve when he describes the dynamics of meter (or *metre* in the French-inflected British spelling):

> Metre is the *primary rhythm*, the organized background against which the *secondary* rhythms of sense and feeling are played out. This is a *crucial* point. You may think that the idea of feeling and thought being subservient to metre is a loopy one. Why should poets build themselves a prison? If they've got something to say, why don't they get on and say it in the most direct manner possible? Well, painters paint within a canvas and composers within a structure. It is often the feeling of the human spirit trying to break free of constrictions that gives art its power and its correspondence to our lives, hedged in as ours by laws and restrictions imposed both from within and without. Poets sometimes squeeze their forms to breaking point, this is what energizes much verse, but if the forms were not there in the first place the verse would be listless to the point of anomie. [*The Ode Less Travelled*, 24–25]

Content

Four Quartets is made up of four self-contained poems, which themselves are divided into five sections, alternating in styles of rhetorical flux and high lyricism. The deployment of imagery, not abstractions, is central to the execution of the poem, and should be allowed to guide the reader/hearer in the experience of the work.

In the second of the *Four Quartets*, "East Coker," Eliot seems to reflect on his life as a poet and the inadequacy of his achievement:

> So here I am, in the middle way, having had twenty years –
> Twenty years largely wasted, the years of *l'entre deux guerres* –
> Trying to learn to use words, and every attempt
> Is a wholly new start, and a different kind of failure
> Because one has only learnt to get the better of words
> For the thing one no longer has to say, or the way in which
> One is no longer disposed to say it.

Of the *Four Quartets*, it is typically recognized that Eliot is reflecting on his own genealogy as a lens through which to consider a larger cultural odyssey. The family that left England from the town of East Coker, arriving on the Dry Salvages off Massachusetts, migrated to the Midwest along Missouri's "strong brown god," only to return in Eliot's person to Little Gidding, a site renowned for its role in English church revival. The pattern suggests this sort of cyclical journey. It is often noted that Eliot also makes use of the four classical elements—air, earth, water, and fire—as a unifying force in the four sections.[11] And, of course, time, the medium through which human life takes place and achieves its salvation or damnation, the same medium in which the incarnation takes place. "East Coker" is the poem of earth and is the earthiest of the poems, speaking of "flesh, fur and faeces," of the rhythms of milking and harvest and conjugal coupling, harkening back to medieval ancestors dancing around the fire, "earth feet, loam feet, lifted in country mirth/Mirth of those long since under earth/

11. Gardner, *The Art of T. S. Eliot*, 43–45.

Nourishing the corn." And there sits Tom Eliot, trying to find the meaning of it all and give it expression of it in a meaningful way. There is a deeply confessional tone to this and all the parts of the *Quartets* which provides the work with a sense of humility. The audience is invited to listen in on this confession and draw what conclusions they see fit for themselves.

In this sense the poem is also a kind of *Divine Comedy* for the modern era; a self-critical review of life, art, and genealogical descent, and a guided purgation of vanity, illusion, and needless despair for the reader. Dante was Eliot's supreme master, of whom he wrote much and alluded to frequently. The poet speaks of the "middle way," of "a dark wood," and of cleansing fire on a journey that leads from despair to resolution, a "condition of complete simplicity," when (quoting the English mystic Julian of Norwich) "all shall be well and . . ."

> All manner of thing shall be well
> When the tongues of flame are in-folded
> Into the crowned knot of fire
> And the fire and the rose are one.

Context

The immediate context of the composition of *Four Quartets* is the Second World War. Eliot had lived *l'entre deux guerres* and no doubt the rising storm of war in the late thirties stimulated Eliot to reflection, much as the First World War had its part in the writing of *The Waste Land*. Eliot had lived through the height of modern confidence and innovation and its ensuing decline with the devastation of the First World War and its repeat in the Second. He had tasted of the confidence, even the arrogance, of European modernity and had come to see its limitations.[12] Beginning in the late

12. Ezra Pound, meanwhile, embraced one of modernity's ideological offspring—fascism—and even engaged in broadcast propaganda for the Mussolini regime. Eliot was tempted, but resisted this siren call and became an ardent supporter of the British monarchy and way of life.

1920s a spiritual turn began to be evident in Eliot's work, as this scion of a Unitarian family came to embrace orthodox Christianity and was received into the Anglican Church.

Eliot was writing a spiritually sensitive artwork in the midst of encroaching European secularism. Reflecting on this very situation, Helen Gardner, writing in the late 1960s, speaks of "the problem of communication for a religious poet in an age where his religious beliefs are not widely held" and how this challenge impinges upon both the content and the craftwork of Eliot's poetry:

> If *Four Quartets* shows skepticism integrated into faith, it shows skepticism none the less; and in a skeptical age it speaks to those whose skepticism stops at the question, and to those who are led to denial, as well as those who are led to believe. It is not the poet's business to make us believe *what* he believes, but to make us believe *that* he believes. He must convince us that he himself is convinced. He must also convince us that what he believes genuinely interprets, makes sense of, experience which we recognize as our own. Although we may not accept his interpretation, we must feel it as a real interpretation. In an age like ours, with no accepted system of belief, in which the traditional system is not so much actively disbelieved as ignored, such an interpretation can only convince if the poet forgoes what earlier Christian writers have loved to employ: the language of the Bible and of the common prayers of the Church.[13]

It has been argued that there was a revival in religious faith following the Second World War with the emergence of Evangelicalism within Protestantism and the renewal of Roman Catholicism with the Second Vatican Council. There is today explicit reference and representation of traditional Christian belief in contemporary works of art and other forms of public discourse, such as films. How effective this is aesthetically is always a matter of debate. But Eliot worked before this post-war revival. His was a time when the aggressive atheism of communism attracted many, especially in certain sectors of the intelligentsia, and when, afterwards, the

13. Gardner, *The Art of T. S. Eliot,* 68.

degradation of the Holocaust caused many to reduce the credible claims of religion to lowest common denominator morality, and the decline in Western "mainline" churches in numbers and cultural prestige was in the offing. In this sense Eliot's light shines all the brighter, even as some today may find his allusiveness and understatement inimical to the kind of full-throated and doubtless forms of religious expression.

Eliot's *Four Quartets* is, in my opinion, the supreme achievement of English language poetry in the twentieth century. It ranks along with and deserves as broad a reception as those other hallmarks of twentieth-century English language masterpieces of Christian imagination: Lewis's *Narnia Chronicles*, Tolkien's *Ring* trilogy, Flannery O'Connor's Southern Gothic stories, Madeleine L'Engle's fantasies, Walker Percy's agrarian novels, and so on. When placed alongside these worthies, we begin to better appreciate the context in which Eliot worked, a twentieth-century modernity at its most assertive and most despairing, caught between the achievements of automation and the horror of atomic war, its aspiration toward a liberalized society alternatingly achieved and thwarted, with unforeseen consequences issuing from both.

EXCURSUS

Helen Louise Gardner (1908–86)

An English literary critic and university teacher, her academic career culminated in her being named the Merton Professor of English Literature at Oxford, the first woman to occupy the chair. A lifelong Anglican, Gardner's Christian faith is subtly but clearly expressed in her writings. Her expertise lay in sixteenth- and seventeenth-century English poetry, particularly that of John Donne, but she also wrote perceptively about her contemporary T. S. Eliot. She was a vocal opponent of French-style literary theory and deconstructionism. She argued against the "rejection of determinate meanings in texts" and insisted that while texts were open to multiple interpretations they remain mediums of intentional communication which readers were advised to try to seek and understand.

While agreeing with Eliot that literature was more than the mere "inculcation of morals," Gardner wrote:

> Since imaginative literature gives us images of human life and records human experience it is inevitably full of moral ideas and moral feelings, strongly engages our moral sympathies, and tests our moral allegiances. But its effects upon us, as a source and a reinforcement of moral values, are often most powerful when indirect and in inverse ratio to the explicitness of an author's moral purpose. Although there is great pleasure in responding to the voice of strong moral conviction, it is not the writers who have a "palpable design upon us" who most notably expand our knowledge of the world and of ourselves, but those who, while they amuse us, evoke our curiosity and engage our sympathies, involve us in a world of moral choice and moral values through our "fond participation" in imagined adventures, crises, joys and distresses. [*In Defense of the Imagination*, 37].

I would simply suggest that what Gardner observes about imaginative literature applies to all forms of art, as I have written throughout this book.

Gardner is generally identified as the basis for the character E. M. Ashford in Margaret Edson's play *Wit*, which was made into a film released in 2001, directed by Mike Nichols and featuring Emma Thompson in the lead role and Eileen Atkins in the role of Ashford.

5

Makoto Fujimura: *The Four Holy Gospels*

In 2009 Makoto Fujimura received a commission by an Evangelical American publishing company to produce a deluxe illuminated edition of the text of the four canonical Gospels in celebration of the four hundredth anniversary of the Authorized Version of the English Bible. Besides extensive marginalia, the project includes five plates, one for each Gospel and one for the front cover, which can stand as works of art in their own right, individually or as a grouping. They represent mature aspects of Fujimura's work, and contain in them much of the arsenal of his style and preoccupations. *The Four Holy Gospels* volume as a whole effectively catalogs Fujimura's techniques, themes, and motifs.

The five plates in order of presentation are *Charis-Kairos* (*The Tears of Christ*), the front cover plate; *Consider the Lilies* (The Gospel according to Matthew); *Water Flames* (The Gospel according to Mark); *The Prodigal God* (The Gospel according to Luke); *In the Beginning* (The Gospel according to John).[1]

As with Eliot's *Four Quartets*, I will proceed with a brief analysis of these five plates following the heuristic model pattern.

---

1. Accesses to full-color reproductions of these five plates are available at http://www.makotofujimura.com/works/the-four-gospels-frontispieces/.

Craft

The craft lying behind Fujimura's art is fundamentally that of watercolor painting. It is, however, of an interesting type and involves unique combinations of aesthetic practice and cultural tradition. He is a practitioner of a form of Asian painting known as *Nihonga*. *Nihonga*, literally "Japanese painting," is a neologism created in the late nineteenth century to distinguish traditional forms of Japanese watercolor-based painting from the primarily oil-based Western-style painting that was then becoming popular and in some ways threatening traditional Japanese practices. By its very nature, *Nihonga* situates Fujimura's art within a traditional mode of visual communication, before matters of particular subjects or commissions are even considered. That mode could be generally described as being naturalistic, understated, and elegant, but further qualification will follow.

To speak of *Nihonga* as a watercolor-based art is true, but requires further specification. *Nihonga* refers to the employment of ink, minerals, and specially prepared pigments, as well as traditional paper canvases and gessoes.[2] The use of thinly cut leaves of gold, silver, and other precious metals is also common. These are applied to paper canvases by means of brushes and other tools unlike those typically used in oil-based painting. Japanese art is also characterized by recurring themes and motifs. This includes landscapes often rendered on large silk-screen panels, giving their often minimalistic renderings a nonetheless impressive feel. Bird-and-flower configurations or *kachō-ga* themes are frequent, along with other naturalistic subject matter. Religious motifs are present, the use of gold leaf adding to a sense of the transcendent. The words of poetry included in art are frequent, underlying the deep connection between the poetry and painting of traditional Japan. "The world of Japanese imagery shimmered with wisteria,

---

2. Gesso, especially in modern art, refers to the white foundation an artist applies to a surface before commencing with a painting. It is a kind of primer.

the seashore, spring rains, spring moon and spring mists, in poetry and painting alike."[3]

Fujimura's art involves these and other aspects of traditional Asian and Japanese aesthetics. His art exudes something hard to pin down, but nonetheless present in Japanese art. One writer captures something of this by way of a contrast to Western art when he writes:

> For [Iwasaki Yoshikazu], the chief characteristic of Western painting and, by extension, Japanese Western-style *yōga* lies in the fact that post-Renaissance tradition in Western art has been focused on the observation of visual realities. On the other hand, the classical Chinese and Japanese traditions have concentrated on an "essentialization," which moves beyond any surface reality in order to locate the essence, most often felt to be a metaphysical essence, of the subject being rendered. By this logic, a Western painter might show us the way a tree looks. A traditional Japanese painter would select elements in the configuration of a real tree in order to show the essence of tree-ness that perforce lies below, beyond the surface reality. Therefore, Iwasaki emphasizes, Western (and Western-style Japanese) painters concentrate on *seeing*, while *Nihonga* artists focus on *feeling*. Intuition, rather than observation, this remains in his view the authentic central concern for painters in the *Nihonga* tradition.[4]

"Intuition, rather than observation," is suggestive of how engagement with such paintings can engender skills and habits of a contemplative consideration with things.

Further complimenting—or complicating—Fujimura's art is his embrace of the aesthetics of abstraction. Abstraction occurs in all art forms, and Japanese art is replete with examples of it from both traditional as well as contemporary sources. But Fujimura was also highly influenced by the tradition of Western abstraction, and most of his work relies on the imaginative logic of this

3. Stanley-Baker, *Japanese Art*, 77. See also Guth, *Art of Edo Japan*, 55–56.

4. Rimer, "Some Final Observations," 74. *Yōga* is the Japanese word denoting Western-style painting.

style of abstract painting. That logic involves the same principles of essentiation that was suggested lies at the root of the traditional Asian aesthetic. Abstraction in both instances seeks to express something metaphysical—or spiritual—about the subject matter at hand.[5]

A note about the "theology" of abstraction may be in order. For some, abstraction represents a flight away from created reality, from reality as it is, as it is given. For this reason many prefer more naturalistic or realistic art on the principle that it somehow honors creation as it is. Moreover such realistic depiction of subject matter seems more straightforward, to the point, unencumbered with complicating theoretical justifications. Artists who engage in abstraction can argue, however, that what we see is not merely what is read off the surface of things, but a conditioned seeing, a seeing through the lens of cultural preoccupations as well as the influence of past art forms and techniques. Abstraction invites viewers to consider what they do indeed see in all things: shapes, colors, gestures. As such it is these elements that perhaps draw us closer to what things essentially are.

Artists working in abstraction also argue that they, like Eliot, cannot simply retrieve and reduplicate the manners and modes of a past art. The conversation, as it were, has moved on. Religious artists of the twentieth and twenty-first centuries often feel that spiritual themes are best approached indirectly, allusively,

---

5. Art historian Julian Bell speaks of the theory of abstraction in early twentieth-century Western art, with particular reference to Wassily Kandinsky's work, relevant to this discussion:

> The visible world had not simply evaporated in this new art. Rather, its essences had been distilled and newly set free, as formulas with which one could build a new pictorial universe. They were none other than those things the eye loves to do: to pick out contrasts, to discern edges and closed shapes, to wander, to zoom and wriggle, to dwell deep in colour intensities, to hurtle and leap sideways. (*Mirror of the World*, 378).

Similarly, David Brown writes of the religious meaning of abstraction for artists such as Kandinsky as a "preoccupation with form and colour as means of highlighting the underlying divine reality of the world"; *God and Enchantment of Place*, 136. See also Kandinsky, *Concerning the Spiritual in Art*.

understatedly. It can be argued that there is a kind of Platonism in works of abstraction, some kind of denial of created reality suggested in the artwork. One can respond, however, that a refined sense of creation can be reaffirmed in abstract art if the artist is inviting viewers to consider the created and inherent value of shapes, colors, gestures, and the materials themselves with which the artists renders the work. There is, of course, no end point in this kind of discussion, only perhaps a widening awareness of the values lying behind different means of communication in art.

Along with the tradition of abstraction in general, however, is Fujimura's deep appreciation for the tradition of an American-style abstract painting, or what is commonly referred to as Abstract Expressionism. Expressionism in any genre of art refers to a preference for the direct expression of emotion and personal perspective at the cost of the usual canons of form and balance. Expressionist art is often characterized by dark, turbulent themes and imagery, especially in its German Expressionist guise of the period following the First World War. American Abstract Expressionism on the whole is a bit more optimistic and jazzy, but still informed and characterized by explorations of the darker psyche. Examples of such include work by Jackson Pollock, Lee Krasner, Mark Rothko, Barnett Newman, and Franz Kline. Expressionist painting places a lot of stock in the power of color and gesture. The "school," such as it was, was also characterized by the use of large-scale canvases, which associated the school with aspirations toward sublimity in their work, suggestive of spiritual themes and outlooks.[6] Fujimura has followed suit in many of his commissions, including large-scale works.

The final element in Fujimura's art, and one that places him in both a unique and a tenuous position in the contemporary art

6. In philosophical aesthetics, the sublime is often contrasted with the beautiful by way of contrasting the terrible and awe-inspiring with the comforting and the reassuring. Abstract Expressionists were often interested in themes of the terrible and awe-inspiring; Rothko, for example, spoke of his own work in terms of expressing fundamental human emotions, "tragedy, ecstasy, doom, and so on." Fujimura has executed large-scale works that invite a similar analysis.

world, is his deep affirmation of Evangelical Christianity. This contributes to a certain tension and drama within his body of work, for his paintings involve the art of his ethnic homeland, where a perception of the vulnerability of this life is central to its aesthetic, as well as the psychological struggles that are so much a part of the Expressionist tradition, employed in the communication of an essentially affirmative worldview rooted in the resurrection of Jesus. Fujimura has developed a sophisticated theo-aesthetic in which the dialectic between the tragic and the affirmative aspects of his adoptive art traditions contribute toward a more full-orbed account of the Christian worldview than is often evident in religious art, art that neither despairs in nor blithely ignores the troubling aspects of human existence.[7] All of this is displayed in the *Four Holy Gospels* project.

Context

As the discussion above of Fujimura's craft suggests, the hybrid nature of his art situates it within a complex of aesthetic and cultural contexts. In another publication, I described this complex as that of a twenty-first-century artist adhering to a medieval tradition of practice in dialogue with twentieth-century perspectives and experiments.[8] Many would identify Fujimura's basic cultural context in terms of an analysis of postmodernism. The term, first occurring in the early part of the twentieth century and originally associated with aspects of architecture, is generally applied to aspects of Western culture and subsequent world culture from the late 1960s onward. For many religious persons, postmodernism is associated with various forms of irrationality, unbounded moral relativism, excessive appeals to categories of race, gender, and social class, and the reduction of all argument to modes of group-think discourse. But positive aspects of postmodernism can be identified from

7. Fujimura has authored several books and chapter contributions where he articulates the aesthetic and philosophical dimensions of his work; see *River Grace*, "That Final Dance," and *Refractions: A Journey of Faith, Art and Culture*.

8. McCullough, "Crises and Resolutions: T. S. Eliot and Makoto Fujimura."

a Christian perspective. Diogenes Allen, who taught for many years at Princeton Theological Seminary, was among the first to articulate how postmodernism actually opened intellectual and affective space for Christian spirituality. Allen suggested that in several important ways postmodernism lifted what he called the "embargo" on faith as a form of legitimate public reason sustained by Enlightenment modernism.[9]

Fujimura is an artist of the postmodern era and a beneficiary of the lifted embargo on public faith which follows in its wake. Being a member of the art world, however, means that he continues to operate professionally under a cloud of suspicion in regards to traditional religiosity, where faith remains associated with ideologically driven violence and illiberal social and moral convictions. It would seem that living in such a precarious and fraught context as the contemporary art world might push artists of faith towards expressions of their vision that are allusive, understated, confident in the powers of suggestion and eschewing bombast and broadcast. There is already an inherent aesthetic of gentleness, understatement, and gracefulness in the choice of artistic methods and materials of traditional Japanese origin. To these Fujimura brings the strength of conviction born of an adult conversion to Christianity and a growing confidence of artistic expression. His art seems at times to be caught between the values of assertion and allusion. In my opinion, his art works best in the postmodern context when its allusiveness is allowed the greater say.

9. Allen, *Christian Belief in a Postmodern World*, 1–19. For a similarly balanced analysis of postmodernism with a focus on the arts see Downing, *How Postmodernism Serves (My) Faith*.

Content

FIGURE 04

Charis-Kairos (The Tears of Christ)

Some aspects of the content of Fujimura's art have already been alluded to in the comments above. I've suggested that a challenge—for some a kind of crisis—is encountered in Fujimura's works for many viewers because of the unfamiliar visual language he employs. By way of reputation and exhibition, viewers are set-up to expect to find Christian themes, only to find what appears to be a cacophony of colors, brushstrokes, and ink stains. Viewers are required to consider meaning not in identifiable representations, but in gestural effects, colors, shapes, and other effects. They are asked to enter into an aesthetic that places greater accent on suggestion rather than representation, or on the representation of something more ethereal rather than a rendition of something visual. This requires a heightened degree of trust that a game is not being played, but that an attempt is being made to connect with a subject matter at its point of epiphenomenal reality. In the case of the *Four Gospels*, they have to trust that the artist sincerely expresses his apprehension of some aspect of each Gospel, and of the gospel itself in the *Charis-Kairos* piece, in these works. That said, many might find the plate accompanying Matthew's Gospel most accessible.

FIGURE 05

The Gospel according to Matthew—Consider the Lilies

At the center of the piece is the faint image of lilies. Derived from a saying of Jesus unique to Matthew's Gospel,[10] its appearance here connects Fujimura's previous usage of traditional Japanese flower motifs in other works with an aspect of the Gospel identified solely with Matthew. The evanescent glory of the flower, which Jesus compares ironically to Solomon's regal glory as a monarch, reflects the ideal of beauty that characterizes Japanese sensitivity towards life. Such a visual "anchor" here may also serve for some as a welcomed presence in an otherwise challenging journey into unfamiliar straights.[11]

The plate associated with Mark's Gospel entitled *Water Flames* may prove particularly challenging. Water flames is a theme linked with a series of paintings Fujimura made immediately following the September 11 events of 2001. His adoption of this theme in relation to Mark's Gospel could be understood on the basis of the way it opens with Jesus' baptism by John, who relativizes his own ministry of water baptism before the one who will baptize with the Spirit (sometimes associated with fire; see Mark 1:6–8). Commenting on this plate Fujimura writes how he sought "to depict the way in which flames not only consume but ultimately sanctify,"[12] a paradox he draws upon frequently in his writings and seems inspired from his reading of Eliot's *Four Quartets*:

10. "And why do you worry about clothing? Consider the lilies of the field, how they grow; they neither toil nor spin, yet I tell you, even Solomon in all his glory was not clothed like one of these" (Matt 6:28–29).

11. Fujimura's explanatory note accompanying the painting underscores both the artistic practice and theological perspective brought to bear in his work. Note should be made of the eschatological emphasis:

> *Consider the Lilies* is done with over sixty layers of finely pulverized precious materials (azurite and malachite), oyster shell white, and painted with sumi ink that has been cured for over a century, as well as gold and platinum powders, and mixed hide glue, to adhere the materials onto the hand-pulled Japanese paper [*kumohada*]. The painting depicts Easter lilies, with triumvirate flowers opening up, but with the suggestion that even these common lilies are transformed into a post-Resurrection, generative reality.
> Fujimura, "Author's Introduction," in *The Four Holy Gospels*, ix.

12. Ibid., xi. Fujimura has based a series of post-9/11 paintings on Eliot's redemption-purgation theme between 2003 and 2006.

The only hope, or else despair
Lies in the choice of pyre or pyre –
To be redeemed from fire by fire.

FIGURE 06

The Gospel according to Mark—Water Flames

The Prodigal God, which prefaces Luke's Gospel, evokes the usage of the "golden mean," the Renaissance method of 3/8 to 5/8 proportionality in a composition, which was suggestive of perfection in the theory of that age. Oriented horizontally, the colors more of earth tones than the rest of the series, the perceptive viewer will find the faint presence of script across the top half of the painting, and an even fainter outline of a human profile.[13]

13. Fujimura's subtle inclusion of words in the painting reflects a frequent

The title of the piece associated it with the similarly named parable found in Luke's Gospel. How is God's prodigality portrayed in this painting? Fujimura, adopting the perspective of his church pastor that "prodigality" means "recklessly spendthrift," seems to want to portray a lavishness of color and design.[14] The text of the eponymous parable, nearly indecipherable, runs from the top of the plate to about 5/8 down. A light brown base freckled with ink marks rises from the bottom, joined 5/8 the way up by a blue and green section shot across with swathes of shell-white and coal-black.

FIGURE 07

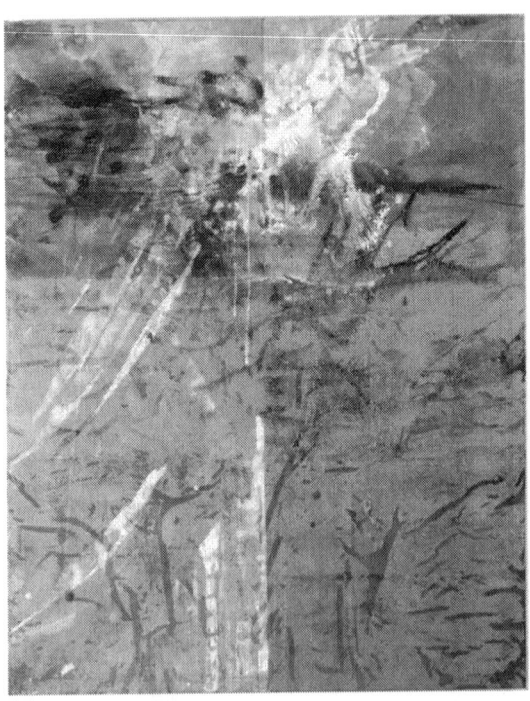

The Gospel according to Luke—The Prodigal God

---

dimension of Japanese art. Joan Stanley-Baker notes how the technique of such "hidden writing" or *ashide* was often used in Japanese art; *Japanese Art*, 86.

14. Fujimura, "Author's Introduction," in *The Four Holy Gospels*, x.

FIGURE 08

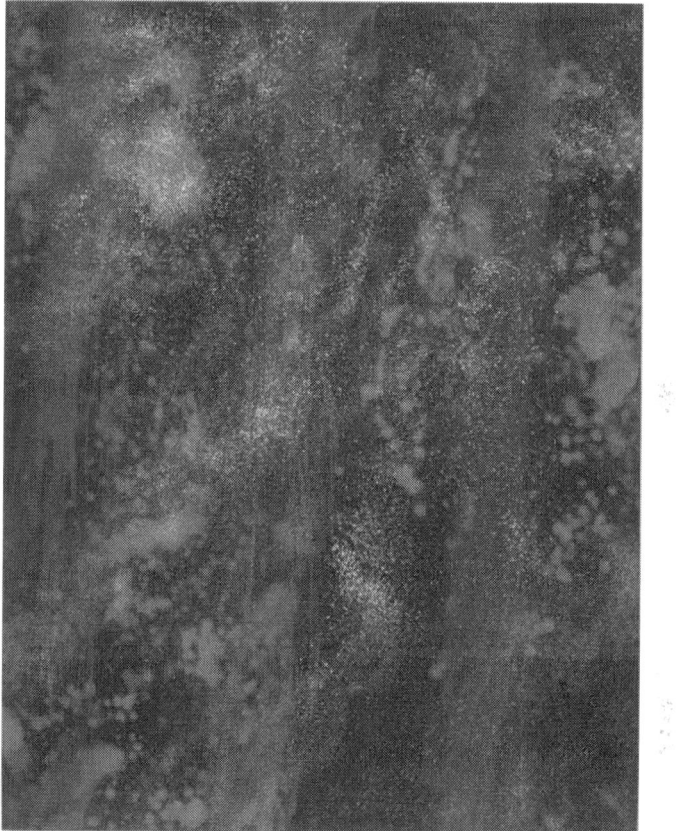

The Gospel according to John—In the Beginning

The plate prefacing John's Gospel returns to the techniques and imagery first encountered in the dramatic front plate, *Charis-Kairos*, and thereby endows the series with a kind of symphonic effect of recapitulation of themes and ideas. By employing similar colors and dynamics in the passion-related first plate with the plate for John, Fujimura may be suggesting the connection between the agency of Logos that brought about creation from chaos and the one who procured redemption by his sufferings. This would certainly serve to advance the incarnational theology of the Fourth

Gospel as well as provide a satisfying sense of unity among the series of plates.

❁

The attentiveness and intuitive thinking "required and released" for a meaningful encounter with art such as Fujimura's may or may not result in "aha" moments of discovery. It may, as already suggested, confirm prior prejudices against abstract art. But it may also inform a new humility before works of unfamiliar provenance and style, and a greater sense of self-openness towards different languages of artistic communication. When James Loder speaks of *interpretation* "of the imaginative solution into the behavioral and /or symbolically constructed world of the original context,"[15] one possibility for many viewers of Fujimura's work is the genuine discovery that after a lifetime perhaps of essentially looking *"through"* paintings in the manner of windows, they need to learn how to look *at* paintings. This is of course the classic definition of modernist painting:

> Reversing the principles of perspective inherited from the 15th century, Cézanne took up Maurice Denis's description of a painting as a "flat surface covered with colours assembled in a certain order," but invested it with a fundamental coherence—using a complex system of colour modulation based on the elimination of outline and flat colour—that was closer to reality. . . . To the problem of depth, Cézanne strove to find a solution based on the modulation of tones. Preparing the way for contemporary painters, he relied on the intrinsic qualities of colour as a tool. For him, line and form were closely linked, with colour determining the fullness of form thorough a fusion of the form-colour and outline functions, and to this the artist added his knowledge of simultaneous contrast. This allowed him to create a sense

15. Loder, *The Transforming Moment*, 34.

of depth through the highly skilful interplay of hard and
soft outlines between his touches of colour.[16]

Art critic Clement Greenberg's mid-twentieth-century
formalist analysis of modern art, which emphasized the surface
dimension of painting, served as a persuasive definition of modern
art for several generations. Fujimura contends that his work exists in a creative tension with that received tradition and invests
his paintings with symbolic significance of the effect of both surface and depth. For many viewers Fujimura's work will be their
first attempt at a sympathetic engagement with "modern" art or
abstraction. The safe space where his work takes place and the as-
sociations between them and recognizable theological and biblical
themes may serve as a doorway toward a whole new perspective
on visual art. When joined with his reflections on art and theology
in various print forms, his entire project can serve as a pedagogy
in theological aesthetics. Indeed, this is what seems to be happen-
ing among the American Evangelicals exposed to his work and
activities.[17]

16. Bernard, *Modern Art: 1905–1945*, 9. David Brown addresses
Cezanne's achievement and the effects it had on subsequent pointing in *God
and Enchantment of Place*, 129–30.

17. Fujimura was featured on the front cover of the influential American
Evangelical magazine *Christianity Today* in its September 9, 2008 issue; see
http://www.christianitytoday.com/ct/2008/september/13.31.html.

EXCURSUS

Mono no aware

Throughout his writings, Makoto Fujimura makes reference to the Japanese notion of *mono no aware*, translated as "the pathos of things" and refers to the artistically inferred vision of life associated with a particular era of Japanese history. "It is emotional shorthand," writes one commentator, "instantly leading from the perception of beauty to a melancholy consciousness of the transience of human life" (Stanley-Baker, *Japanese Art*, 83). It remains an identifiable aspect of Japanese culture. Fujimura himself writes:

> *Mono no aware*, a Japanese expression that captures the sentiment of sorrow (literally "sorrow of things"), points to the notion of beauty as sacrifice. In order for people to enjoy the feast at a banquet, a sheep must be sacrificed. Autumn leaves are most beautiful and bright as they are distressed with their impending death. The minerals I use in my paintings must be pulverized to bring out their true beauty. Art serves this kind of sacrificial beauty, and art should be redefined to consider the relational acts as much as products we produce to communicate. [*Refractions*, 54].

It would be wrong to infer or suggest that Fujimura's paintings are "sad," but that his art consciously seeks out signals of the transcendent in the midst of pain and paradox.

6

James MacMillan:
Seven Last Words from the Cross

THE CONTEMPORARY SCOTTISH COMPOSER James MacMillan burst onto the British concert music scene with *The Confession of Isobel Gowdie,* a piece for large orchestra premiered in 1990. Since then he has had a succession of featured premieres of orchestral, instrumental, and choral works. Among his many commissions includes a fanfare for the opening of the first Scottish parliament in July of 1999, and he continues to receive commissions in a remarkably prolific career. MacMillan is a committed Roman Catholic who has spoken publicly about his faith. Many of his vocal and choral works are settings of traditional Latin texts. In the same year that the Scottish parliament was reconvened MacMillan gave an impassioned speech on what he felt is the continuing presence on anti-Catholic prejudice in Scotland.

MacMillan has yet to receive sustained attention in the United States, although his works have been performed by major instrumental and choral organizations around the country. His work warrants attention as it exhibits several features of contemporary composition.[1]

1. Michael Capps provides a helpful overview of Macmillan's music and reception in America in "Warld in a Roar."

Craft

MacMillan is a composer working within the contours of Western music as it has been inherited from the period of Gregorian Chant through the experiments of twentieth-century modernism. His mature style could best be described as eclectic, drawing upon the resources suggested in the spectrum of time outlined above. As such, many would identify his style as being postmodern, of which more will be said below. Many of his works are explicitly designed for ecclesiastical use, as well as for public events, and for the concert hall.

MacMillan has been identified with "holy minimalism," a designation MacMillan has accepted, but it isn't particularly accurate for many of his more recent works. As one commentator noted:

> unlike his populist minimalist or "religious-minimalist" contemporaries, [MacMillan] has not completely rejected the modernism of his youth. Complex atonality often exists alongside lucid tonality or modality; the language is as likely to be acerbically or punchily dissonant as coolly or sweetly modal.[2]

MacMillan acknowledges his aim to produce music that is accessible to contemporary listeners, while eschewing a kind of commercial populism. MacMillan writes critically of what he considers to be the elitism of serious twentieth-century music and of its apparent disdain for popular accessibility. Two things seemed to have turned MacMillan aesthetically and made way for the works that have now garnered him critical and popular acclaim. One is politics. MacMillan is drawn toward matters of justice, where powers of evil seek to and sometimes do inflict great suffering on innocent people. These themes are explored in works like *Búsqueda* (1988), based on poems by mothers of the "disappeared" in Latin American conflicts, and the aforementioned *Confession of Isobel Gowdie*, which focuses on the unjust imprisonment and extracted confession of a woman in seventeenth-century Scotland. This sort

2. Johnson, "James MacMillan," 514.

of concern for the common person elicits a desire on MacMillan's part to write music accessible to the average concertgoer.[3]

The other influence is his identification with Catholic Christianity. It seems to be MacMillan's intention to make accessible, to represent in a "vernacular" musical language, the object of Christian faith. It is MacMillan's stated intention to bridge what had previously been presented to him as separated spheres of human experience, the religious and the political, the artistic and the popular, through his compositions. It is also significant to note MacMillan's preoccupation with unjust human suffering and the experience of Jesus. MacMillan himself acknowledges his preoccupation with the events of the Triduum, the three days of Jesus' passion and resurrection.[4] For MacMillan, the two areas reflect and illuminate each other: the experience of human injustice is mirrored and redeemed in the injustice visited upon the Son of God. For MacMillan, these are themes not to be confined within the walls of "museum" music, but expressed in ways that are both substantial and accessible. Thus, MacMillan's music is characterized by "exuberantly colourful, with dashes of reassuringly familiar dance-band harmonies, and glittering with theatrical virtuosity that has to be seen to be believed."[5]

3. MacMillan, "God, Theology and Music," 16.

4. Ibid., 20.

5. Daniel Jaffé, "James MacMillan," http://www.compositiontoday.com/articles/james_macmillan_interview.asp. In an email exchange with the author, musicologist George Harne articulates an opposing perspective on MacMillan's work in a way that reflects Harne's ongoing commitment to musical modernism as well as the influence of Frankfort School social criticism. His critique highlights one thesis of this project, that art is implicated in its context and responsible for its modes of communication:

> My rejection of MacMillan's music rests on his regressive use of tonality. Tonality has become so commodified through the mass media (both the chordal structures and gestures) that its use by a serious composer today would be like a serious poet creating (unironically) a poem based on Hallmark greeting card clichés. So there is the question of commodification but also that of the historicity of musical material. No matter how much we might wish to, we cannot return to the musical language of the past. This is not novelty for novelty's sake or a devotion to the god of innovation. God made us creatures of time, which makes us subject to history. Our cultural creations are also subject to history. [December 4, 2009].

Excursus

The Language of Music

One of the key features of Western music is the dynamic of tension and resolution. Western music moves according to harmonic progressions, and at certain moments the music builds toward a point where we naturally expect and even desire resolution. This includes, but is not restricted to, "grand finales" in a given piece, and is true even in the progressions in radio pop songs. We may sense it in terms of the resolution of a verse or stanza, but the harmonic progression of the song generally underscores this movement with a corresponding move from suspension to resolution, a feeling that the phrase has satisfyingly concluded. This harmonic drive toward resolution gives Western music it's "sense of an ending" or its strong sense of *teleology*, that it is going somewhere. The triadic harmony that we are familiar with took hold in Western music during the late Renaissance, and it is a part of our musical language, which we largely take for granted.

Western music is also characterized by melodies, motives, and themes that, especially since the Baroque period, were the subjects of all manner of development, further underscoring the teleological sense of Western music.

The kind of innovations that took place in music during the twentieth century were attempts to change this language. The German modernist composer Karlheinz Stockhausen (1928–2007) described characteristic features of Western music and the avant-garde resistance to it when he wrote:

> No repetition, no variation, no development, no contrast. All these presuppose "figures"—themes, motives, objects—which are repeated, varied, developed, and contrasted; dissected, manipulated, magnified, reduced, modulated, transposed, mirrored or retro-graded. *All that has been given up . . . our world—our language—our grammar.* [Jeremy Begbie, *Music in God's Purposes*, 11].

Context

As suggested above, MacMillan, like Fujimura, has lived and practiced his art in the bridge period between the modernism and the postmodernism of Western culture. Like Fujimura, MacMillan engages in dialogue with, sometimes in diatribe against, the musical modernism of the twentieth century. Much of twentieth-century concert music is characterized with the breaking down of traditional modes of form, harmony, and melody and their replacement with new forms of utterance. One might think of the atonality of Arnold Schoenberg,[6] the extremely acerbic music of Anton Webern, the repetitive minimalism of Philip Glass, the dissonances employed by Elliott Carter, or the experimentation of Steve Reich and John Cage, works that contemporary concert bills usually sandwiched between more popular and accessible works. This is not at all to suggest that these composers are "bad" by their association with these compositional trends. For aesthetic and even spiritual reasons composers sought new forms and content in the same way that painters explored the breaking down of traditional visual representations and subjects matters in the twentieth century.[7]

But as in all human endeavors certain orthodoxies set in, in this case demanding that for music to have integrity it must resist easy accessibility. MacMillan rejects this premise in part, as suggested above, because of the elitism it evinces. MacMillan is not alone in this quest for modes of musical composition commensurate with the themes and values he wishes to communicate. In an article published in 2000, MacMillan writes how:

> in the last 10 years or so a number of composers have bucked [the modernist] trend. Composers like John Tavener, Henryk Górecki, and Arvo Pärt have been taken into the affections of a larger music loving public, not always the traditional older classical music audience

6. Schoenberg actually preferred the word "pantonality" to describe his technique. See Dika Newlin, *Bruckner, Mahler, Schoenberg*.

7. For a fine account of twentieth-century music, see Ross, *The Rest Is Noise: Listening to the Twentieth Century*.

but a new audience of younger people. Some might say disparagingly that it is a nineties new age audience that has taken to the mysticism and the simplicities of the likes of Tavener, Górecki and Pärt. Why are we seeing such a flourishing of spiritual composers at this time? The music of these three composers on the face of it is very beautiful, it is music which avoids the complexities common in a lot of contemporary, avant-garde, modernist music of the twentieth century. There is a return to some sense of modality, if not tonality, and there is an ethereal atmosphere in their music that I think makes people relax and feel vaguely spiritual. There seems to be a hunger for something to fill the spiritual void and some of this music at least gives people a kind of folk memory of what spiritual sustenance was about.[8]

Recalling Eliot's earlier proposal that modern poetry must be allusive and "dislocating," twentieth-century composers who followed aesthetic values would make a counterargument. Again, these are the debates that are part of contemporary art world conversations. In any case, appreciating MacMillan's music involves understanding its position within developments that took place within the twentieth century. Its immediate postmodern context is one where, especially in choral music, religious texts and themes remain and in some ways are the only sources of new and vital works in this genre. Apart from works for the operatic stage, one has to think long and hard to identify compelling new choral works expressing purely secular sentiments or convictions.

8. MacMillan, "God, Theology and Music," 16. Musicologist Kurt Sander writes similarly of this resurgence:

We are now witnessing a new public penchant of the metaphysical in the arts. The music of composers like John Tavener, Ivan Moody, Giya Kancheli, and Henryck Gorecki have acquired considerable attention recently, but have been carelessly termed "new simplicity" or "holy minimalism" in an attempt to explain with recycled tags their anomalistic appearances at the end of the 20th century. [Sanders, Book Review: *Arvo Pärt*, by Paul Hillier, http://www.arvopart.org/article.php?id=41].

Content

As suggested above, the content of much of MacMillan's music focuses on themes of the redemptive potential of unmerited suffering. Sometimes compared to the work of his late contemporary John Tavener (1944–2013), MacMillan has been called a composer of the cross. As with the Japanese cultural and aesthetic aspects of Fujimura's work, such descriptions serve as handy points of entrance, but should not be made into sufficient descriptions of a large and varied body of work. The work I have chosen, however, fits neatly in this characterization.

SEVEN LAST WORDS FROM THE CROSS (1993)

The earliest musical settings of the Seven Last Words date to the early sixteenth century. Heinrich Schütz (1585–1672) composed a setting in the seventeenth century, and Joseph Haydn composed what is perhaps the best known setting in the eighteenth. Nineteenth-century examples were composed by Charles Gounod and Caesar Franck. The setting of the sayings of Jesus from the cross, as recorded in each of the Four Gospels, comes from efforts to form means by which meditation on and affective identification with Jesus and his suffering could be enhanced. Other such examples would be the Christmas nativity or crèche and the Stations of the Cross.

MacMillan calls his work a "cantata for choir and strings." By calling it a *cantata*, MacMillan is simply signaling it as a multi-movement vocal work.

To Janis and Tony as a wedding gift

SEVEN LAST WORDS
FROM THE CROSS

JAMES MACMILLAN
(b. 1959)

I. Father, forgive them for they know not what they do

11005

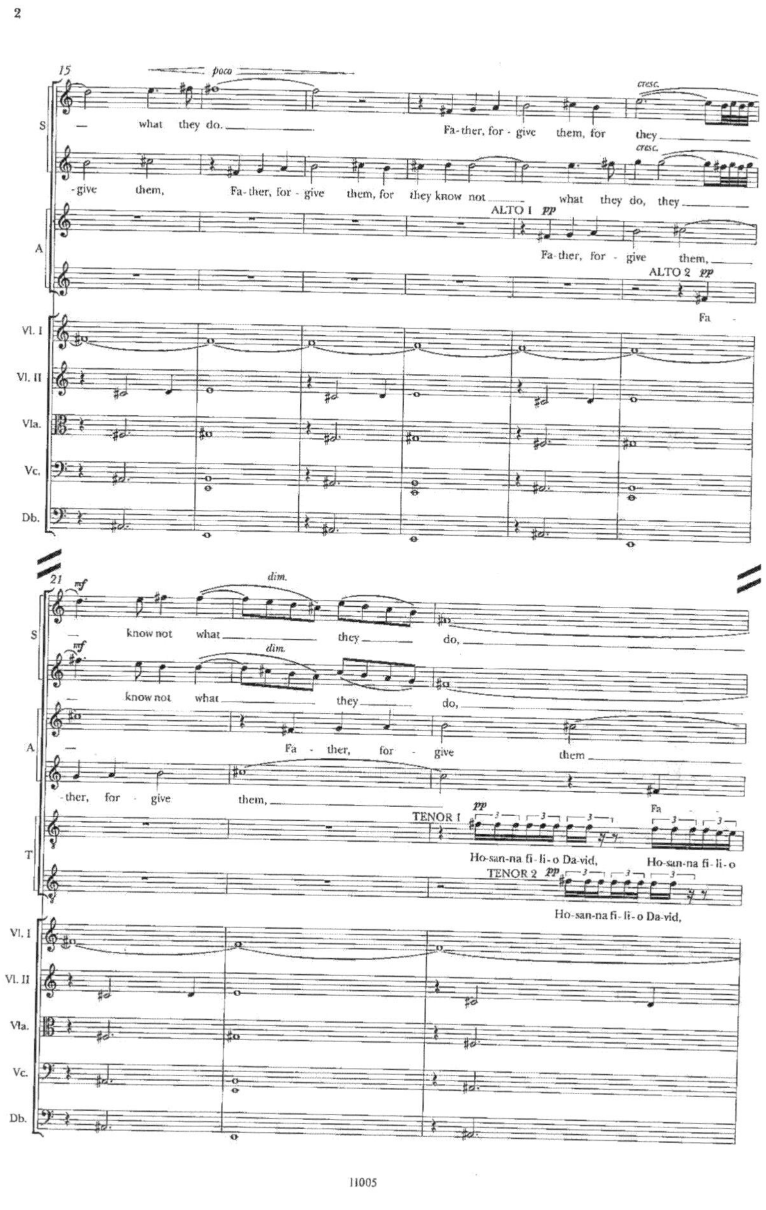
2
15
poco
what they do.
Fa-ther, for-give them, for they
cresc.
-give them, Fa-ther, for-give them, for they know not what they do, they
ALTO I pp
Fa-ther, for-give them,
ALTO 2 pp
Fa-
S
A
Vl. I
Vl. II
Vla.
Vc.
Db.
21
mf
dim.
know not what they do,
Fa-ther, for-give them
-ther, for-give them,
Fa
TENOR I pp
Ho-san-na fi-li-o Da-vid, Ho-san-na fi-li-o
TENOR 2 pp
Ho-san-na fi-li-o Da-vid,
T
11005

MacMillan arranged the text for this choral work with string orchestra accompaniment. The traditional seven sayings form the core of the text, but MacMillan intersperses selections from Roman Catholic liturgical sources associated with the triduum (that is, the three days from Maundy Thursday evening to Easter Sunday). Much of what characterizes MacMillan's music is found in here, including a basic tonality textured with moments of dramatic dissonance, hints of chant along with the kind of "ornamented" vocal writing that characterize his music.

The work opens with a slow, three-note ascending motive which is taken up and developed by the sopranos into an ascending scale in the Phrygian mode. MacMillan's use of this ancient church mode gives the piece its archaic feel, while the orchestral accompaniment provides a dissonant underscoring, giving the music its frisson between the old and the new. The short ascending motive reappears in various configurations, creating a sense of unity throughout the seven-movement work. With the exception of a movement that uses duet soloists, the entire piece is for the choir, sometimes in split sections, allowing for up to eight lines of choral music to occur simultaneously, giving MacMillan opportunity to display remarkable contrapuntal skills.

The overall effect of the cantata can be likened to a Greek tragic chorus, commenting on the spectacle before them. There is no soloist singing the role of Jesus, so members of the chorus sing the words from the cross, along with the texts that MacMillan has chosen. The sharp articulation possible with string instruments is brought to bear in passages of a jarring, piercing quality. Great poignancy is created with a solo violin obbligato in one movement, while the injustice of the passion is expressed in fortissimo passages of choral singing. The interpolated texts from liturgical sources focus attention on Jesus as the rejected sufferer. Part of the text for the first movement which MacMillan chose from the Good Friday Responsaries captures much of what is expressed in the music:

The life that I held dear I delivered into the hands of the
    unrighteous
and my inheritance has become for me like a lion in the forest.
My enemy spoke out against me,
"Come gather together and hasten to devour him."
They placed me in a wasteland of destruction,
and all the earth mourned for me.
For there was no one who would acknowledge me or give me
    help.
Men rose up against me and spared not my life.[9]

Even for most first-time listeners, MacMillan's music will
be accessible. What may be new is the tradition of the Seven Last
Words and its intended design to foment a heightened affective
engagement with the events and meaning of Good Friday. The suffering of Jesus, his passion, is a central aspect of Roman Catholic
piety that may be new for Christians from different church back-
grounds. MacMillan's efforts in this work might be likened to the
use of the crucifix in Catholic church decoration and personal
adornment or Mel Gibson's intentions in producing his 2004 film
The Passion of the Christ. Spending extended time in meditation
on the passion and deferring the relief and resolution of Easter
may represent a new experience for some. Johann Sebastian Bach
of course produced his great St. Matthew Passion (as well as a St.
John Passion and the B Minor Mass), but in doing so Bach reflects
his historical proximity to the kind of Catholic piety and forms of
worship his grandparents would have been familiar with. Protes-
tants of various communions have, of course, a wealth of hymns
that reflect on Jesus' death and which form a counterpart to the
Seven Words and Stations of the Cross traditions. It could be argued, however, that many forms of contemporary Protestantism
tend to reflect what Martin Luther called a "theology of glory" at
the expense of a theology of the cross. Works like this by Mac-
Millan may be one way of redressing this imbalance, as well as

9. MacMillan, *Seven Last Words from the Cross*, CD liner booklet.

developing new capacities in musical attentiveness and emotional engagement with a point of faith and doctrine.

Recommended Recordings

Below is a selective discography of works by composers mentioned in this chapter. All are recent recordings, and most available on the inexpensive but reliable Naxos label.

James MacMillan, *Seven Last Words from the Cross*, Naxos 8.570719, performed by The Dmitri Ensemble under Graham Ross. MacMillan himself endorses this recording of the work.

Other works by noted members of the "holy minimalists" include:

Henryk Górecki, *Symphony No. 3 (Symphony of Sorrowful Songs)*, *Three Olden Style Pieces*, Naxos 8.550822, performed by the Polish National Radio Orchestra under Antoni Wit. *Symphony No. 3* gained wide popularity in Britain and is a wonderful elegy on the tragedies of the twentieth century.

Arvo Pärt, *Alina*, ECM New Series 1591, 449958-2. This CD includes the extremely minimalistic piece for violin and piano entitled "Spiegel im Spiegel," which has garnered much popular attention through its uses in several film soundtracks.

Arvo Pärt, *Tabula Rasa, Symphony No. 3, Collage*, Naxos 8.554591, performed by the Ulster Orchestra under Takuo Yuasa. Excellent recording of minimalism in an orchestral guise.

Arvo Pärt and John Tavener, *Out of the Night*, Sony Classical SK 61753, performed by the Taverner Choir under Andrew Parrott. This fine recording includes choral music by these two composers of note.

John Tavener, *Song for Athene, Svyati and Other Choral Works*, Naxos 8.555256, Performed by the Choir of St. John's College, Cambridge under Christopher Robison. Selection of thirteen of Tavener's best known choral works, including the piece sung at the funeral of Princess Diane. An excellent introduction to Tavener's music.

7

Conclusion: What Are They Saying?

I have staked much of the value of this project on the claim that the arts are means of communication, that through the employment of craft and the manipulation of content an artist *"says"* something, and that it is integral to the full engagement, understanding, and enjoyment of art that its viewers or readers or hearers break through to this point of communication with the artwork, and by extension with the artist or the tradition out of which it emerges. So it seems incumbent on me to provide some sense of what I at least believe the artists explored in this section are saying in these particular examples of their work.

Two qualifications need to be restated. One is that the engagement with art is reduced and perhaps ruined if one seeks to simply take away a "message." Art is an irreducible amalgam of *what* is said and *how* it is said, to the point that they are inseparable. For analytic purposes, however, one can tease them apart in order to better appreciate the amalgamation achieved in the artwork. Second, a particular artwork can and should be enjoyed and explored on its own terms and merits, but a sense of its fuller import is gained when the particular work is situated within the artist's larger body of work. As Helen Gardner puts it in relation to literature:

> [A]lthough at any moment we are reading a single work, that work is usually part of an *oeuvre*, which we either know in part or can get to know. As we read more and

> more of an author's work we can come to know a way
> of regarding the world of human experience, a mode of
> expression, and an individual idiom that is characteristic
> of all his works however various they may be.[1]

I believe that this principle applies to all art forms. With this said, let me make some suggestions which I trust reflect an *informed opinion* of the works under consideration.

Let us begin with Eliot. It seems to me that the poet in the *Four Quartets* provides a big clue as to what he is saying by prefacing the work with Greek epigraphs from Heraclitus. As translated by Gardner, the first text reads, "Although the Word is common to all, most men live as if each had a private wisdom of his own."[2] The second epigraph Eliot himself renders in the poem as "the way up is the way down."[3] The poem seems to speak to what Gardner calls "religious truth" expressed in the allusive manner Eliot felt aesthetically necessary and Gardner commends as appropriate in a secular age.[4] The Word (Greek *logos*) is common to all. Most folks miss it. Recovering one's capacity to recognize it requires a sometimes paradoxical journey or sustained reflection upon one's life. Such a self-reflexive journey involves purgation, a cleansing of the heart and mind, a journey in the time of one's personal life as well as one's ancestral life. Such is what Eliot's poem seems to be communicating.

What is Fujimura saying in the five plates from the *Four Holy Gospels* project? Whatever else these particular paintings are saying about the subject matters that they address, Fujimura's art is about the inherently sensuous and beautiful qualities of the materials with which he works and the possibilities for new beauty latent in their combination and organization. Those pigments, those broken shells and pulverized minerals, reflect a transcendent beauty immanent in this world, a beauty still present in, or even enhanced by, a pulverizing process. An association of this process

1. Gardner, *In Defense of the Imagination*, 7.
2. Gardner, *The Art of T. S. Eliot*, 61.
3. Eliot, "The Dry Salvages," in *Collected Poems: 1909–1962*, 196.
4. Gardner, *The Art of T. S. Eliot*, 61.

with the sufferings of Christ becomes plausible. Fujimura also stipulates that painting such as his invites the viewer to consider again the depths of things; bucking trends and theories of twentieth-century painting, Fujimura uses the qualities of his materials and their application to create images of both depth and surface. Fujimura frequently cites a celebrated passage from William Blake that underscores the kind of mystical appropriation of things suggested in his work:

> To see a World in a Grain of Sand
> And a Heaven in a Wild Flower,
> Hold Infinity in the palm of your hand
> And Eternity in an hour.[5]

Such seeing and (be)holding requires those ascetic virtues of patience, attentiveness, imaginative reconfiguration, and dialogue that have been suggested throughout this book. Fujimura's art is one such occasion to exercise these skills and open oneself up to new ways of considering pictorial representation.

So much of James MacMillan's music speaks to how suffering releases redemptive potential in the world, and this is clearly the case again in "Seven Last Words." All three works explored in this section could be said to have external reference points that shape one's appropriation of their meaning: musical form in the case of Eliot, the Gospels in Fujimura, and the passion in MacMillan. Yet in all three we "come to know a way of regarding the world of human experience" with different emphases. Were we to explore a greater variety of examples we would no doubt encounter a wider range of perspective, but since all three are Christians they share a common resource for their perspective on the human experience. That common resource is the *story* into which all three, in their own ways, invite their audiences to try out, to indwell, to affirm, to question, to consider. Their telling of the Christian story is inflected in different ways because of differing historical, national, ethnic, aesthetic, and ecclesial contexts, but it is identifiably the same

---

5. Blake, "Auguries of Innocence," as quoted in Fujimura, *River Grace*, 4.

story "of the one Annunciation."[6] Time spent with artworks such as these can help Christians develop "the capacities and dispositions to think, feel, and act in accordance with their worldview no matter what the circumstances"[7] by assisting them in an *indwelling* of the story. Art brings into *focal* attention what lies *subsidiarily* in the heart and mind, through which Christians have been evaluating and understanding their world but not always aware of the full implications. Art raises to fresh awareness the beauty, the poignancy, and the pathos of the faith in a world that tends toward arid rationalization or crass sensationalism.

6. Eliot, "The Dry Salvages," in *Collected Poems: 1909–1962*, 195.

7. Lindbeck, "Spiritual Formation and Theological Education," 287.

Part III

Conclusion

8

Eyes that See, Ears that Hear

But blessed are your eyes, for they see, and your ears, for
they hear.[1]

The epigraph for this final chapter is taken from Matthew's account
of the parable of the Sower. Jesus spoke in parables, a profoundly
aesthetic mode of communication. Parables make their appeal to
the imagination and operate along the same lines as all the arts: as
forms of reason that make their argument in terms of analogies,
comparisons, contrasts, proportions, suggestions, and insinuations. The genius of the parables (one can also think of some bril-
liant examples from the Old Testament as well) is the way in which
they ascertain from the listener an agreement in principle, if not
in practice. Emily Dickinson captures the metaphorical logic of
parables and of art in general when she writes:

> Tell all the truth but tell it slant—
> Success in Circuit lies
> Too bright for our infirm Delight
> The Truth's superb surprise
> As Lightning to the Children eased
> With explanation kind
> The Truth must dazzle gradually
> Or every man be blind—[2]

1. Matt 13:16
2. Dickinson, "Tell All the Truth," public domain.

Karl Barth, and more recently Timothy Gorringe, suggest that parables hold promise as one way of perceiving the theological value of art. It is a commendable move in as much as it highlights the aesthetic nature of the parables and helps those new to the arts to recognize the metaphorical properties of art. On the other hand, it can also lend itself to affirming predetermined judgments of art based on theological criteria, or (even worse) the reduction of art to its perceived "message." In the present case, however, I am simply drawing on parables as examples of artistry in order to restate my basic thesis, that capacities for sensory perception have a certain analogical or, even better, a dialectical relationship with capacities for spiritual perception. Capacities in the one can strengthen and foment capacities in the other. There are many ways that the sensory and spiritual faculties can be dialectically strengthened; the arts are one way that this relationship can be *catalyzed*. In relation to this I have presented a dynamic analysis of the arts as products of craft, content, and context in order to open up the ways in which arts are forms of reason employing learned skills and conventions of communication as well as being unique and original utterances that carry the residue of their times and pick up the residues of their new environs. The arts are products that can be *read*, whose arguments can be followed, and which produce experiences of beauty in their isomorphic union of *what* is said and *how* it is said.

Closely related to this kind of analysis of parables is that applied to the dynamic of narrative. I, along with many others, am convinced that the best way to understand ourselves, our beliefs, and our worldviews is in terms of *story*. I hardly need to contribute to the large body of literature written for general readership as well as the academy on this subject. My contention is that all artistic utterances begin from and invite audiences into some story-informed sense of being. Some argue for this perspective descriptively. Karen Smith for example writes:

> Story has power not only to evoke memory, to unite, to give identity and purpose, but it may also have *the power to call us to a different way of being*. When we least expect

it, we may find story breaking into the mundane and ordinary: to shape, to cleanse, to heal and to transform. Stories help us make sense out of life. They help us to shape our understanding of what is and what is not. They enable us to become. They speak to us of what we are and are not yet and in this way, they serve to remind us of an uncompleted present.[3]

Lisa Hess employs new participles when she writes how a "storying way of knowing" underscores the ineluctably communal dimension of all epistemology as well as the notion that knowing involves practices and not mere subject matter mastery.[4] Drawing similarly on a Polanyian understanding of personal knowledge, James Sire writes:

> To indwell a story is to live so much within its framework that we are not so conscious of the story as of what the story allows us to see. Indwelling is like using a telescope. When we look through a telescope, we see things that we cannot see with the naked eye, but we do not "see" the telescope. Rather we *indwell* the instrument in order to do what we could not otherwise do, to see things we otherwise could not see.[5]

Such indwelling through an artwork, living "within its framework," however briefly or long, is a key aspect of meaningful encounter. The capacity to do so is born of *aesthetic* experiences and ascetic practice, the combination of which has potential to enrich both dimensions of life. In this project I have been concerned to make the connection between *aesthesis* and *ascesis*, between sensory perception and spiritual discipline. It is a profoundly difficult thing to de-center one's self, to still the hum of self-preoccupation, and open one's self to something new and unfamiliar, something challenging, perhaps even threatening or familiar and reassuring for a fresh consideration. The capacity to do so requires of many people a kind of training to resist distraction, to focus

3. Smith, *Christian Spirituality*, 46. Emphasis added.

4. Hess, *Artisanal Theology*, 68.

5. Sire, *Naming the Elephant*, 105.

concentration, to suspend judgment, and to give oneself over to someone else or something else in order to receive communication, perspective, or point of view. Borne over a long-term course of practice, people growing into such capacities are characterized by their poise, their attentiveness, their ability to be fully present with another person or object of study. They bear the characteristics of the contemplative. They have qualities that we might attribute in some circumstances to a *saint*. David Benner, a practicing Christian therapist, writes:

> [T]he essential dynamic of the human spirit is a radical drive for self-transcendence: a longing to be more than we are, to be all we can be. At some deep level we seem to recognize this "more" is not simply more of the same but that it demands deep transformation. It involves a reorganization of the self so radical that our old self must be released before our new and larger self can unfold. We must, as Jesus taught, be prepared to lose our life if we wish to truly gain it. Transformation always involves a continuing series of surrenders of the smaller selves to which we attach ourselves as we become larger and more authentic. These acts of letting go form the transitional moments on the journey—the moments where our response to the inner call of self-transcendence results in the quantum shifts in our center of gravity that I have described as the movement from one level of consciousness to another.[6]

This book argues that Benner's notion of a "continuing series of surrenders" can be facilitated, among other ways, by meaningful encounters with art. Art, which Aidan Nichols relates to rhetoric when he writes of it as "a kind of address,"[7] has been analyzed as a communicative phenomenon embodied in the form of the various "languages" of learned crafts and practices, the significance of which is identified as the nexus of its form and content, which is both implicated and received within historical and situational contexts that bear upon the "reading" of or encounter with the

6. Benner, *Spirituality and the Awakening Self*, 191.

7. Nichols, *The Art of God Incarnate*, 93.

artwork. Artworks instantiate themselves within a matrix of values and perspectives, analyzed here in terms of its "story," its "world-projection," the truth-claims of which are insinuated in showing the implications of its claims as opposed to a mere broadcasting of them. The encounter with art as described here can be enhanced by, and sometimes requires, a kind of tutorial in its language and historical context. But when encountered in meaningful ways—that is, ways in which the artwork's world-projection is encountered —artworks can alter the understanding of things and experience of the world. David Harned, as we have seen, accents the ethical dimension of this dynamic:

> Some men make the artifacts that we call works of art. They are created for many of the same reasons effective in the development of language. They initiate us more fully to the particularity of things and situations we confront and the emotions we feel.[8]

Conclusion

It is probably clear to the reader that the originality of this book, such as it is, lies in the synthesizing of various strands of thought into a new model for the relationship between the arts and human experience, namely that of religious formation. The central thesis guiding this project is that dynamic spirituality lies in the mutually shaping interface of learned skills involving sensory reception and perception and learned skills of attentiveness, curiosity, concentration, willingness to change one's point of view, and so forth, capacities related spirituality or to what one author calls the "long obedience in the same direction."[9] The realm of the arts, it is argued, can serve as one effective field wherein these dialectical, mutually informing capacities can be catalyzed. Spiritual formation comes about through looking and looking. And listening. And watching. And waiting. And reading. Over and over again. On the

---

8. Harned, *Theology and the Arts*, 30.

9. Peterson, *A Long Obedience in the Same Direction.*

other hand, meaningful and loving encounters with the arts can be complimented and even enriched with the input of the kind of contemplative capacities associated with religion and spirituality.

Bibliography

Allen, David G. "Aesthetic Perception in Mikel Dufrenne's *Phenomenology of Aesthetic Experience.*" *Philosophy Today* 22.1 (1978) 50–64.

Allen, Diogenes. *Christian Belief in a Postmodern World: The Full Wealth of Conviction.* Louisville: Westminster John Knox, 1989.

————. *The Path of Perfect Love.* Boston: Cowley, 1987.

————. *Spiritual Theology: The Theology of Yesterday for Spiritual Help Today.* Boston: Cowley, 1997.

Allen, Diogenes, and Eric O. Springsted. *Philosophy for Understanding Theology.* Louisville: Westminster John Knox, 2007.

Anfam, David. *Abstract Expressionism.* World of ArtLondon: Thames and Hudson, 1996.

Apostolos-Cappadona, Diane. "On Seeing *The Passion*: Is There a Painting in This Film? Or Is This Film a Painting?" In *Re-Viewing The Passion: Mel Gibson's Film and Its Critics*, edited by S. Brent Plate, 97–108. London: Palgrave, 2004.

Arnheim, Rudolf. *Art and Visual Perception: The New Version.* Berkeley: University of California Press, 1974.

————. *Visual Thinking.* London: Faber and Faber, 1970.

Astley, Jeffrey, et al., eds. *Theological Perspectives on Christian Formation: A Reader on Theology and Christian Education.* Leominster, UK: Gracewing, 1996.

Austin, Michael. *Explorations in Art, Theology and Imagination.* London: Equinox, 2005.

Baal-Teshuva, Jacob. *Rothko: Pictures as Drama.* Cologne: Taschen, 2003.

Baggley, John. *Doors of Perception: Icons and Their Spiritual Significance.* Crestwood, NY: St. Vladimir's Seminary Press, 1988.

Bartholomew, Craig G., and Michael W. Goheen. "Story and Biblical Theology." In *Out of Egypt: Biblical Theology and Biblical Interpretation*, edited by Craig Bartholomew, Mary Healy, Karl Möller, and Robin Parry, 141–75. Carlisle, UK: Paternoster, 2004.

Bashō, Matsuo. *The Narrow Road to the Deep North and Other Travel Sketches.* Translated by Nobuyuki Yuasa. London: Penguin, 1966.

————. *On Love and Barley: Haiku of Basho*. Translated by Lucien Stryk. London: Penguin, 1985.

Begbie, Jeremy. "Christ and the Cultures: Christianity and the Arts." In *The Cambridge Companion to Christian Doctrine*, edited by Colin E. Gunton, 101–19. Cambridge: Cambridge University Press, 1997.

————. "Jeremy Begbie on Beauty." www.transpositions.co.uk/2013/04/jeremy-begbie-on-beauty.

————. *Music in God's Purposes*. Edinburgh: Handsel, 1989.

————. *Theology, Music and Time*. Cambridge Studies in Christian Doctrine. Cambridge: Cambridge University Press, 2000.

————. *Voicing Creation's Praise: Towards a Theology of the Arts*. London: T & T Clark, 1991.

Bell, Julian. *Mirror of the World: A New History of Art*. London: Thames and Hudson, 2007.

Benner, David G. *Spirituality and the Awakening Self: The Sacred Journey of Transformation*. Grand Rapids: Brazos, 2012.

Benner, Juliet. *Contemplative Vision: A Guide to Christian Art and Prayer*. Downers Grove, IL: IVP, 2011.

Benson, Bruce Ellis. *Liturgy as a Way of Life: Embodying the Arts in Christian Worship*. Grand Rapids: Baker Academic, 2013.

Bernard, Edina. *Modern Art: 1905–1945*. Paris: Chambers, 2004.

Bownas, Geoffrey, and Anthony Thwaite. *The Penguin Book of Japanese Verse: From the Earliest Times to the Present*. London: Penguin, 2009.

Burnham, Scott. *Beethoven Hero*. Princeton: Princeton University Press, 1995.

Brown, David. *Discipleship and Imagination: Christian Tradition & Truth*. Oxford: Oxford University Press, 2000.

————. *God and Enchantment of Place: Reclaiming Human Experience*. Oxford: Oxford University Press, 2004.

————. *God and Grace of Body: Sacrament in Ordinary*. Oxford: Oxford University Press, 2007.

————. *God and Mystery in Words: Experience through Metaphor and Drama*. Oxford: Oxford University Press, 2008.

————. "In the Beginning was the Image." Unpublished paper delivered at the Society for the Study of Theology, 2010.

————. *Tradition and Imagination: Revelation and Change*. Oxford: Oxford University Press, 1999.

Brown, David, and Ann Loades. *The Sense of the Sacramental: Movement and Measure in Art and Music, Place and Time*. London: SPCK, 1995.

Brown, Frank Burch. *Good Taste, Bad Taste, and Christian Taste: Aesthetics in Religious Life*. Oxford: Oxford University Press, 2000.

————. *Religious Aesthetics: A Theological Study of Making and Meaning*. London: Macmillan, 1990.

Brown, Jeannine K. *Scripture as Communication: Introducing Biblical Hermeneutics*. Grand Rapids: Baker Academic, 2007.

Capps, Michael. "Warld in a Roar: The Music of James MacMillan." *Image* 54 (Summer 2007) 95–105.

Carey, John. *What Good Are the Arts?* London: Faber and Faber, 2005.

Carroll, Noël. *Art in Three Dimensions.* Oxford: Oxford University Press, 2010.

Cooke, Deryck. *The Language of Music.* London: Oxford University Press, 1959.

Collingwood, R. G. *The Principles of Art.* London: Oxford University Press, 1938.

Conant, Ellen P. *Challenging Past and Present: The Metamorphosis of Nineteenth-Century Japanese Art.* Honolulu: University of Hawai'i Press, 2006.

———. *Nihonga, Transcending the Past: Japanese-Style Painting, 1868–1968.* St. Louis: The St. Louis Art Museum, 1995.

Cunningham, Lawrence S., and Keith J. Egan. *Christian Spirituality: Themes from the Tradition.* Mahwah, NJ: Paulist, 1996.

Dalrymple, John. *Longest Journey: Notes on Christian Maturity.* London: Darton, Longman and Todd, 1979.

Dickie, George. *Art and Value.* Malden, MA: Blackwell, 2001.

Downing, Crystal L. *How Postmodernism Serves (My) Faith: Questioning Truth in Language, Philosophy and Art.* Downers Grove, IL: IVP, 2006.

Dutton, Denis. "A Naturalist Definition of Art." *The Journal of Aesthetics and Art Criticism* 64 (2006) 367–77.

Dyrness, William A. *Poetic Theology: God and the Poetics of Everyday Life.* Grand Rapids: Eerdmans, 2011.

———. *Senses of the Soul.* Eugene, OR: Cascade, 2008.

Eliot, T. S. *Collected Poems, 1909–1962.* London: Faber & Faber, 1963.

———. *Old Possum's Book of Practical Cats.* San Diego: Harcourt Brace and Co. 1939.

Elkins, James. *On the Strange Place of Religion in Contemporary Art.* New York: Routledge, 2004.

Farley, Edward. *Faith and Beauty: A Theological Aesthetic.* Aldershot, UK: Ashgate, 2001.

Ford, Leighton. *The Attentive Life: Discerning God's Presence in All Things.* Downers Grove, IL: IVP, 2008.

Fry, Stephen. *The Ode Less Travelled: Unlocking the Poet Within.* London: Arrow, 2007.

Fuchs, R. H. *Dutch Painting.* London: Thames and Hudson, 1978.

Fujimura, Makoto. "Artist's Introduction." In *The Four Holy Gospels, English Standard Version (ESV),* ix–xii. Wheaton, IL: Crossway, 2011.

———. *Refractions: A Journey of Faith, Art and Culture.* Colorado Springs, CO: NavPress, 2009.

———. *River Grace.* East Greenwich, RI: Meridian, 2007.

———. "That Final Dance." In *It Was Good: Making Art to the Glory of God,* 2nd ed., edited by Ned Bustard, 296–300. Baltimore: Square Halo, 2006.

Gardner, Helen. *The Art of T. S. Eliot.* London: Faber & Faber, 1968.

———. *In Defense of the Imagination.* Cambridge: Harvard University Press, 1982.

―――. *The Metaphysical Poets*. New York: Penguin, 1972.

Gaut, Berys, and Dominic McIver Lopes, eds. *The Routledge Companion to Aesthetics*. 2nd ed. Routledge Philosophy Companions. London: Routledge, 2010.

Gombrich, E. H. *Art and Illusion: A Study in the Psychology of Pictorial Representation*. 1959. Reprint. Oxford: Phaidon, 1980.

―――. *The Story of Art*. 16th ed. Oxford: Phaidon, 2006.

Goodman, Nelson. *Languages of Art: An Approach to a Theory of Symbols*. London: Oxford University Press, 1969.

―――. *Ways of Worldmaking*. Edinburgh: Harvester, 1978.

Gorringe, Timothy. *Earthly Vision: Theology and the Challenges of Art*. New Haven: Yale University Press, 2011.

Graham, Gordon. "Learning from Art." *The British Journal of Aesthetics* 35 (1995) 26–37.

―――. *Philosophy of the Arts: An Introduction to Aesthetics*. 3rd ed. London: Routledge, 2005.

Grootenboer, Hanneke. *The Rhetoric of Perspective: Realism and Illusionism in Seventeenth-Century Dutch Still-Life Painting*. Chicago: University of Chicago Press, 2005.

Guth, Christine. *Art of Edo Japan: The Artist and the City 1615–1868*. New Haven: Yale University Press, 1996.

Guthrie, Steven R. *Creator Spirit: The Holy Spirit and the Art of Becoming Human*. Grand Rapids: Baker, 2011.

Hanfling, Oswald. *Philosophical Aesthetics: An Introduction*. Oxford: Blackwell, 1992.

Harned, David Baily. *The Ambiguity of Religion*. Philadelphia: Westminster, 1968.

―――. *Creed and Personal Identity: The Meaning of the Apostles' Creed*. Edinburgh: Handsel, 1981.

―――. *Faith and Virtue*. Edinburgh: St. Andrew, 1973.

―――. *Grace and Common Life*. Charlottesville: University Press of Virginia, 1971.

―――. *Images for Self-Recognition: The Christian as Player, Sufferer, and Vandal*. New York: Seabury, 1977.

―――. *Patience: How We Wait upon the World*. Boston: Cowley, 1997.

―――. *Strange Bedfellows: Growing up with India*. Bangalore: Ultra, 2010.

―――. *Theology and the Arts*. 1966. Reprint. Eugene, OR: Wipf & Stock, 2014.

Harries, Richard. *Art and the Beauty of God: A Christian Understanding*. London: Mowbray, 1993.

Harrison, Charles. *An Introduction to Art*. New Haven: Yale University Press, 2009.

Hart, David Bentley. *The Beauty of the Infinite: The Aesthetics of Christian Truth*. Grand Rapids: William B. Eerdmans, 2003.

Hauerwas, Stanley. "The Significance of Vision: Toward an Aesthetic Ethic." *Sciences Religieuses/Studies in Religion* 2 (1972) 36–49.

Hein, David, and Edward Henderson. *C. S. Lewis and Friends: Faith and the Power of Imagination.* Eugene OR: Cascade, 2011.

Herrick, James A. *The History and Theory of Rhetoric: An Introduction.* Boston: A & B, 2005.

Hess, Lisa M. *Artisanal Theology: Intentional Formation in Radically Covenantal Companionship.* Eugene, OR: Cascade, 2009.

———. *Learning in a Musical Key: Insight for Theology in Performative Mode.* Princeton Theological Monography Series. Eugene, OR: Pickwick, 2011.

Hibbs, Thomas S. *Rouault/Fujimura: Soliloquies.* Baltimore: Square Halo, 2009.

Hirsch, Edward. *How to Read a Poem: And Fall in Love with Poetry.* San Diego: Harcourt, 1999.

Howes, Graham. *The Art of the Sacred: An Introduction to the Aesthetics of Art and Belief.* London: I. B. Tauris, 2010.

Jaffé, Daniel. "James MacMillan." December 4, 2009. http://www.composition today.com/articles/james_macmillan_interview.asp

Johnson, Stephen. "James MacMillan." In *The New Grove Dictionary of Music and Musicians,* edited by Stanley Sadie, 20 vols., 15.514–15. London: Macmillan, 2001.

Jones, Cheslyn, et al. *The Study of Spirituality.* London: SPCK, 1986.

Kandinsky, Wassily. *Concerning the Spiritual in Art.* Translated by M. T. H. Sadler. 1914. Reprint. New York: Dover, 1977.

Kermode, Frank, ed. *Selected Prose of T. S. Eliot.* San Diego: Harcourt, 1975.

Lewis, C. S. *An Experiment in Criticism.* Cambridge: Cambridge University Press, 1961.

———. *Studies in Words.* Canto Classics. Cambridge: Cambridge University Press, 1990.

Lindbeck, George. "Spiritual Formation and Theological Education." In *Theological Perspectives on Christian Formation: A Reader on Theology and Christian Education,* edited by Jeff Astley et al., 299–305. Grand Rapids: Eerdmans, 1996.

Loder, James E. *The Logic of the Spirit: Human Development in Theological Perspective.* San Francisco: Jossey-Bass, 1998.

———. "Transformation in Christian Education." In *Theological Perspectives on Christian Formation: A Reader on Theology and Christian Education,* edited by Jeff Astley et al., 271–85. Grand Rapids: Eerdmans, 1996.

———. *The Transforming Moment: Understanding Convictional Experiences.* San Francisco: Harper & Row, 1981.

Louth, Andrew. *The Origins of the Christian Mystical Tradition: From Plato to Denys.* Oxford: Clarendon, 1981.

Lyall, David. *The Integrity of Pastoral Care.* New Library of Pastoral Care. London: SPCK, 2001.

MacMillan, James. "God, Theology and Music." *New Blackfriars* 81.948 (2000) 16–26.

———. *Seven Last Words from the Cross.* CD liner booklet. The Dmitri Ensemble. Graham Ross. Recorded March 27th–29th, 2008. Naxos 8.570719, 2009, compact disc.

Masterpieces of Chinese and Japanese Art. Freer Gallery of Art Handbook. Washington, DC: Smithsonian Institute, 1976.

McGinn, Bernard, and John Meyendorff, ed. *Christian Spirituality: Origins to the Twelfth Century.* London: Routledge and Kegan Paul, 1986.

McGrath, Alister E. *Christian Spirituality: An Introduction.* Oxford: Blackwell, 1999.

McCullough, James. "Aesthesis and Ascesis: The Relationship between the Arts and Spiritual Formation." PhD diss., University of St. Andrews, 2013.

———. "Crises and Resolutions: T. S. Eliot and Makoto Fujimura." *Qu4rtets*, edited by Gregory Wolfe, 59–66. New York: The Fujimura Institute, 2012.

Meek, Esther Lightcap. *Loving to Know: Covenant Epistemology.* Eugene, OR: Cascade, 2011.

Meskin, Aaron. "From Defining Art to Defining the Individual Arts: The Role of Theory in the Philosophies of Arts." In *New Waves in Aesthetics*, edited by Katherine Stock and Katherine Thompson-Jones, 125–49. New York: Palgrave MacMillan, 2008.

Miles, Margaret. *Image as Insight: Visual Understanding in Western Christianity and Secular Culture.* Boston: Beacon, 1985.

Monti, Anthony. *A Natural Theology of the Arts: Imprint of the Spirit.* Aldershot, UK: Ashgate, 2003.

Mayer, J. D., et al. "Emotional Intelligence as Zeitgeist, as Personality, and as Mental Ability." In *The Handbook of Emotional Intelligence: Theory, Development, Assessment, and Application at Home, School, and in the Workplace*, edited by Reuven Bar-On and James D. A. Parker, 92–116. San Francisco: Jossey-Bass, 2000.

Mudge, Lewis S., and James N. Poling. *Formation and Reflection: The Promise of Practical Theology.* Philadelphia: Fortress, 1987.

Nichols, Aidan. *The Art of God Incarnate: Theology and Image in Christian Tradition.* London: Darton, Longman and Todd, 1980.

———. *A Key to Balthasar: Hans Ur von Balthasar on Beauty, Goodness, and Truth.* Grand Rapids: Baker Academic, 2011.

———. *Lost in Wonder: Essays on Liturgy and the Arts.* Aldershot, UK: Ashgate, 2011.

———. *Redeeming Beauty: Sounding in Sacral Aesthetics.* Aldershot, UK: Ashgate, 2007.

Newlin, Dika. *Bruckner, Mahler, Schoenberg.* New York: Kings Cross, 1947.

Nouwen, Henri, with Michael J. Christensen and Rebecca Laird. *Spiritual Formation: Following the Movements of the Spirit.* London: SPCK, 2011.

O'Kane, Martin, ed. *Imaging the Bible: An Introduction to Biblical Art.* London: SPCK, 2008.

Osmer, Richard R. *Practical Theology: An Introduction.* Grand Rapids: Eerdmans, 2008.

Osmer, Richard R., and Friedrich L. Schweitzer, eds. *Developing a Public Faith: New Directions in Practical Theology.* St. Louis, MO: Chalice, 2003.

Pattison, George. *Crucifixions and Resurrections of the Image: Christian Reflections on Art and Modernity.* London: SCM, 2009.

Pattison, Stephen. "Spirituality and Spiritual Care Made Simple: A Suggestive, Normative and Essentialist Approach." *Practical Theology* 3 (2010) 351–66.

Pearcey, Nancy. *Saving Leonardo: A Call to Resist the Secular Assault on Mind, Morality, and Meaning.* Nashville: B&H, 2010.

Peterson, Eugene. *A Long Obedience in the Same Direction: Discipleship in an Instant Society.* Downers Grove, IL: IVP, 2000.

Phillips, Glenn, and Thomas Crow. *Seeing Rothko.* Los Angeles: The Getty Research Institute, 2005.

Porter, Jean. "Virtue." In *The Oxford Handbook of Theological Ethics*, edited by Gilbert Meilaender and William Werpehowski, 205–219. Oxford: Oxford University Press, 2005

Porter, Steve. "Sanctification in a New Key: Relieving Evangelical Anxieties over Spiritual Formation." *The Journal of Spiritual Formation and Soul Care* 1.2 (2008) 129–48.

Principe, Walter. "Theological Trends: Pluralism in Christian Spirituality." *The Way* 32 (1992) 54–61.

———. "Toward Defining Spirituality." *Sciences Religieuses/Studies in Religion*, 12 (1983) 127–41.

Resniak, Valerie. "Contemporary Spirituality." In *The New SCM Dictionary of Christian Spirituality*, edited by Philip Sheldrake. London: SCM, 2005.

Rimer, J. Thomas. "Some Final Observations." In *Nihonga: Transcending the Past*, edited by Ellen P. Conant, 72–74. St. Louis, MO: St. Louis Art Museum, 1995.

Romaine, James, ed. *Art as Spiritual Perception: Essays in Honor of E. John Walford.* Wheaton, IL: Crossway, 2012.

Ross, Alex. *The Rest is Noise: Listening to the Twentieth Century.* New York: Picador, 2007.

Rothko, Mark. *Writings on Art.* Edited by Miguel López-Remiro. New Haven, CT: Yale University Press, 2006.

Schaeffer, Francis A. *Art and the Bible.* Downers Grove, IL: IVP, 1973.

Scruton, Roger. *Understanding Music: Philosophy and Interpretation.* London: Continuum, 2009.

Sherry, Patrick. *Images of Redemption: Art, Literature, and Salvation.* London: T & T Clark, 2003.

———. *Spirit and Beauty*, 2nd ed. London: SCM, 2002.

Sheldrake, Philip. "Spirituality and Healthcare." *Practical Theology* 3.3 (2010) 367–79.

———. *Spirituality and History: Questions of Interpretation and Method.* London: SPCK, 1995.

Shults, F. LeRon. *Reforming Theological Anthropology: After the Philosophical Turn to Relationality.* Grand Rapids: Eerdmans, 2003.

Shults, F. LeRon, and Steven J. Sandage. *Transforming Spirituality: Integrating Theology and Psychology*. Grand Rapids: Baker Academic, 2006.

Siedell, Daniel A. "Art and the Practice of Evangelical Faith—A Review Essay." *Christian Scholars Review* 34.1 (2004) 119–31.

———. *God in the Gallery: A Christian Embrace of Modern Art*. Grand Rapids: Baker Academic, 2008.

Simmonds, Gemma. "Spiritual Formation," In *The New SCM Dictionary of Christian Spirituality*, edited by Philip Sheldrake, 329–40. London: SCM, 2005.

Sire, James. *Apologetics beyond Reason: Why Seeing Really is Believing*. Downers Grove, IL: IVP, 2014.

———. *Naming the Elephant: Worldview as a Concept*. Downers Grove, IL: IVP, 2004.

Smart, Alastair. "Has Shock Art Lost Its Bite?" *Seven: The Sunday Telegraph Weekly Magazine*, March 4 , 2012.

Smith, Karen E. *Christian Spirituality*. SCM Core Text. London: SCM, 2007.

Stangos, Nikos, ed. *Concepts of Modern Art: From Fauvism to Postmodernism*. World of Art. London: Thames and Hudson, 1994.

Stanley-Baker, Joan. *Japanese Art*. World of Art. London: Thames and Hudson, 2000.

Stock, Katherine, and Katherine Thompson-Jones, eds. *New Waves in Aesthetics*. New Waves in Philosophy. New York: Palgrave Macmillan, 2008.

Thayer, Nelson S. T. *Spirituality and Pastoral Care*. Theology and Pastoral Care. Edited by Don S. Browning. Minneapolis: Fortress, 1985.

Thornton, Martin. *English Spirituality: An Outline of Ascetical Theology According to the English Pastoral Tradition*. 1986. Reprint. Eugene, OR: Wipf and Stock, 2012.

Vanhoozer, Kevin J. *Is There a Meaning in This Text?: The Bible, the Reader, and the Morality of Literary Knowledge*. 1988. Reprint. Grand Rapids: Zondervan, 1998.

———. "Praising in Song: Beauty and the Arts." In *The Blackwell Companion to Christian Ethics*, edited by Stanley Hauerwas and Samuel Wells, 112–23. Malden, MA: Blackwell, 2006.

Viladesau, Richard. *Theology and the Arts: Encountering God through Music, Art and Rhetoric*. Mahwah, NJ: Paulist, 2000.

Walford, E. John. *Jacob van Ruisdael and the Perception of Landscape*. New Haven, CT: Yale University Press, 1991.

Wallace, Mark I. "The New Yale Theology." *Christian Scholar's Review* 27 (1987) 154–70

Walton, Kendall. "Aesthetics—What? Why? and Wherefore?" *The Journal of Aesthetics and Art Criticism* 65 (2007) 147–61.

Watkins, James. "Review: *Echoes of Eden*." http://www.transpositions.co.uk/2014/05/review-echoes-of-eden/

Weil, Simone. *An Anthology*. Edited by Siân Miles. London: Penguin, 2005.

Williams, Rowan. *Grace and Necessity: Reflections on Art and Love*. London: Continuum, 2005.

Wilson, Jonathan R. "From Theology of Culture to Theological Ethics: The Hartt-Hauerwas Connection." *The Journal of Religious Ethics* 23 (1995) 149–64.

Wiseman, James A. *Spirituality and Mysticism: A Global View*. Maryknoll, NY: Orbis, 2006.

Wright, Dana R., and John D. Kuentzel. *Redemptive Transformation in Practical Theology: Essays in Honor of James E. Loder, Jr.* Grand Rapids: Eerdmans, 2004.

Wright, N. T. *The New Testament and the People of God*. London: SPCK, 1992

Yasumura, Toshinobu. *Rimpa: Decorative Japanese Painting*. Tokyo: PIE, 2011.

Zuckerkandl, Victor. Review of *The Language of Music*, by Deryck Cooke. *Journal of Music Theory* 4 (1960) 104–9.

Recommended Reading

Theological Aesthetics

David Brown is producing some of the most penetrating and wide-ranging scholarship related to theology, art, and culture. New readers may want to begin with his 2004 *God and Enchantment of Place*, where he articulates his basic theses and project.

Brown, David. *Tradition and Imagination: Revelation and Change*. Oxford: Oxford University Press, 1999. Brown introduces his controversial thesis, that the Christian tradition, including the meaning of Scripture, is an ever-moving phenomenon and that God, through a dialectical process involving received revelation and cultural innovation, continues to disclose fresh truths and insights. The arts are seen here as a vital part of this cultural dynamic. Reflections on the meanings of the Pentecost and nativity narratives over time, as revealed in art, may be especially interesting to readers.

———. *Discipleship and Imagination: Christian Tradition and Truth*. Oxford: Oxford University Press, 2000.

———. *God and Enchantment of Place: Reclaiming Human Experience*. Oxford: Oxford University Press, 2004. Introduces Brown's thesis that God makes Himself available through means of grace, inside and outside of what are generally considered "religious" sources today. Painting, landscape, architecture, and athletics are considered, replete, as are all five volumes, with many examples.

———. *God and Grace of Body: Sacrament in Ordinary*. Oxford: Oxford University Press, 2007. This volume continues the exploration in relation to the human figure in art and music in its classical, popular, blues, and operatic guises.

———. *God and Mystery in Words: Experience through Metaphor and Drama*. Oxford: Oxford University Press, 2008. Concludes this project with explorations in the use of metaphor in poetry, hymnody, drama, and choral music.

Brown, Frank Burch. *Religious Aesthetics: A Theological Study of Making and Meaning.* London: Macmillan, 1990.

Harries, Richard. *Art and the Beauty of God: A Christian Understanding.* London: Mowbray, 1993. An excellent introduction for the general reader on the relationship of beauty and its manifestation in art and the Christian life.

Painting and Iconography

Baggley, John. *Doors of Perception: Icons and Their Spiritual Significance.* Crestwood, NY: St. Vladimir's Seminary Press, 1988. An excellent introduction to this feature of Orthodox faith and practice for the general reader.

St. John of Damascus. *Three Treatises on the Divine Images.* Translated by John Behr. St. Vladimir's Seminary Press Popular Patristic Series. Crestwood, NY: St. Vladimir's Seminary Press, 2003. The first and greatest statement on the theology of iconography. Everyone cites it, this is a fine translation, you might as well read it.

Siedell, Daniel A. *God in the Gallery: A Christian Embrace of Modern Art.* Grand Rapids: Baker, 2008. As the subtitle suggests, an affirmative exploration of modern art, its theories, and concrete examples. Argues against forms of "soft iconoclasm" and for an enlargement of Protestant theology that can accommodate the challenges and opportunities of contemporary art.

Poetry and Literature

Gardner, Helen. *The Art of T. S. Eliot.* London: Faber and Faber, 1968 (reprinted 1991). The classic statement on Eliot's work, and a rewarding exploration of poetry in general.

Sire, James W. *How to Read Slowly: Reading for Comprehension.* Colorado Spring: WaterBrook, 1978. A fine guide for reading literature and poetry meaningfully. Sire has been a primary advocate for "worldview analysis" and rational apologetics, but had been strangely reluctant to include aesthetics as part of his analytic and apologetic efforts. This appears to be changing with the publication of his new book *Apologetics beyond Reason: Why Seeing Really is Believing* (Downers Grove, IL: IVP, 2014).

Music

Begbie, Jeremy S. *Theology, Music and Time.* Cambridge: Cambridge University Press, 2000. Somewhat technical, but still an accessible exploration of how music illustrates theological claims and incarnates God's Trinitarian Being in our dimension of space and time.

Spirituality and Spiritual Formation

Hess, Lisa M. *Artisanal Theology: Intentional Formation in Radically Covenantal Community*. Eugene, OR: Cascade, 2009.
———. *Learning in a Musical Key: Insight for Theology in a Performative Mode*. Eugene, OR: Pickwick, 2011. Both volumes provide wonderful insights and definitional creativity about spirituality, spiritual formation, and theological wisdom in relation to creativity and artistry.
Nouwen, Henri, with Michael J. Christensen and Rebecca J. Laird. *Spiritual Formation: Following the Movements of the Spirit*. New York: HarperCollins, 2011. Nouwen was noted for many writings on spirituality and pastoral theology. This book, edited from previously unpublished material, explores the spirituality of the human life cycle. Of particular interest for theological aesthetics is book's use of the idea of *visio divina* as a compliment to the more familiar *lectio divina*. Chapters include practical steps for "sacred looking" as a spiritual exercise.